God's Cookin'

and the

Devil's

Well Done!

Rose Leibundguth

Ginny

Col. 1, 2, 3

Love,
Mova

God's
Cookin'
and the
Devil's
Well Done!

Rose   Leibundguth

"GOD's COOKIN' *and the* **𝒟evil's WELL DONE!"**

ISBN #1-931262-01-2
LCCN #2001099461

© 2002 Rose Leibundguth Ministries

All Scripture is from the Amplified Bible Version unless otherwise noted.

Published by *Mercy House* / Rose Leibundguth Ministries
Box M
Burgin KY 40310

Rose Leibundguth Ministries
Burgin, KY

Contents

INTRODUCTION

GOD's COOKIN' *and the* ✐**evil's WELL DONE!** One of the greatest books ever written about Jesus *and* you! In this thrilling book, long hidden truths are revealed about your love, your faith-walk, your peace with Jesus, and His love for you. As you read, you will grow strong! As your heart hungers for a clearer knowledge of your rights and privileges in Christ, we urge you to read ... to feast upon the courageous, exciting words in ...

GOD's COOKIN' *and the* ✐**evil's WELL DONE**

I want you to *know* ... **GOD's COOKIN'** *and the* ✐**evil's WELL DONE! Jesus Is Lord all around you,** *and* **in you!**

You have the faith of Jesus! Circumstances and Satan are not lord over you! And although Satan roams about the earth, lying, looking for who he *may* devour ... Jesus came to live inside you, to make you free! You have His Faith ... His abundant life!

Father God gives us life in abundance, to prosper, to be in good health *and* enjoy, even as our soul prospers!

I can confidently tell you today, you *have* Jesus, and you *have* His abundant Life to walk in! You can stop fearing, and worrying! You can leap forward; you can get past your past!

As ministers of the gospel, we are entrusted with God's strength and might. We are therefore faced with two responsibilities:

1. To develop and maintain excellence of ministry
2. To deal with Satan and minister God's love and Word.

Excellence in ministry absolutely will not tolerate unbelief, failure or "taking the easy way out." It is time for us to rejoice and enjoy our life in Jesus! It is time for us to know that we are forgiven and cleansed by Jesus *and* forgive ourselves! It is time for us to *know* that we *know* Jesus!

2000 years ago, Jesus, at His blessed victorious death and resurrection, eternally paralyzed and defeated Satan in the pit of hell!

God's Glorious Victories are everywhere! **Jesus Is Lord!**

Jesus Is Love!

Today, God in His consistent, infinite Love, Grace and Mercy still moves every mountain into the sea ... **every mountain!**

ALL mountains, by God's Grace are moved ... are gone forever!

In the mountain moving faith and love of Jesus, Satan is forever reminded he's a paralyzed and defeated enemy!

But, the devil wants to make you *look* at circumstances! Satan wants you to fear, doubt, feel hopeless and alone, be despaired, feel unloved, and be defeated! Satan wants you fooled and buried, bowed down to him, to disasters ... buried under mountains of hopelessness!

As we dance with *The King*, we learn to dance in glory on the devil's head victoriously from mountaintop to mountaintop.

My desire is to introduce to you how to dance with your King Jesus ... your King of Victory and Love ...

Because *in Jesus*, in God's Word, you find out that you are not a loser. *In Jesus*, you are **Dressed to Win ...** a victorious winner!

When we *look to* our feelings or *look at* our circumstances ... instead of Jesus or His Love and Word for us ... we open that big door for Satan to sow seeds of fear, doubt, and discouragement into our minds, and hearts! When we speak fear and doubt into our circumstances, instead of Jesus, we are cursing God! Then Satan can sow *and* grow his evil seeds of hopelessness, and despair! Satan wants to use us to curse our Lord!

Jesus has already met every need you could ever have according to *all* His riches in glory! In the Great Victory of Jesus, learn how you can talk, walk, and dance with Jesus as your mountain remover, "Need Meeter" ... your victory team mate.

Further, I will show you in God's Word that we are **God's Beloved** ... Jesus is alive living on the inside of us! We can take hold of Jesus living inside us! We can walk our victory walk with Jesus!

We can learn how to take back all Satan has stolen from us!

Ask! Ask Jesus! Jesus will help you and tell you what to do about every circumstance and question in your life.

He says in His Word, *"I have your path prepared before you — walk over it in My Faith, My Love, My Hope, and My restful Victory for you! I love you ... you can trust Me! I will never leave you or forsake you!"*   Psalms 16:11; Acts 2:25-28, 31

As you read, learning that **You Are God's Beloved Creation** ... you will begin to look only into the Forgiving, Beautiful Eyes of Jesus! You will learn to know,

JESUS IS your King ...

your trustworthy Provider ...

your sweet Love ...

your abundant Healer ...

your powerful Protector ...

your strong Joy ...

your complete Redeemer ...

your total Peace ...

your personal Savior ...

your all powerful Lord ...

your Good Shepherd ...

your Forgiveness ...

your "Faith Builder" ...

your victorious, rich Deliverer!

Jesus and your Father God joyfully lead you and supply you. Jesus will never, never leave you or forsake you!

This astounding book, prompted by the Holy Spirit, teaches us, *"We are free in Jesus!"* Nothing Satan can think up or throw at us can harm us!

Keep looking at Jesus *as you* walk in your victory walk with your King Jesus!

We walk in His abundant freedom and victory … Jesus!

We can have God's victorious Word over-flowing in our hearts and minds! Enjoy praising Jesus … meditating day and night on His Word.

Welcome Beloved, to this Holy Spirit inspired book, with me, a blessed Child of God!

We pray that your fellowship, your relationship with the Lord, your walk in the Spirit … your intimacy with the Father deepens as you read afresh the Words God has given me, a blessed lady! I desire for you to intimately know Jesus! I desire for you to know His abundant, rich love, and life for you!

Enjoy reading this exciting book as you walk, talk and live in the Good News of your victory in Jesus as your loving, living Christ!

Holy Child of God, Jesus will change your life forever as you hear and act on God's glorious truths, His Love, and revelations from His Word for you.

We give all praise and glory to Father God and Jesus Christ! He sends the Holy Spirit to inspire Children of God everywhere like myself!

Listen to Jesus! Praise God and Rejoice! We are walking in the greatest time ever known on this planet earth, ever known to mankind, ever known in this Universe!

I Love you as the Father,

Rose

Mercy House / Rose Leibundguth Ministries

God's Cookin'
and the
Devil's
Well Done!

Rose Leibundguth

Rose Leibundguth

CHAPTER 1

JESUS IS THE TRUTH
~
SATAN IS THE LIAR

HONEY, THE LOVE OF JESUS IS EXTRAVAGANT!

THE *TRUTH* OF JESUS *and* THE BIBLE, GOD'S WORD,
REVEALS THE DEFEATED,
EVIL ENEMY — SATAN!

We *have* Jesus! HE *is* The Truth! John 14:6

THERE IS A SATAN! HE IS THE LIAR!

John 8:44, *"... the devil ... he was a murderer from the beginning and does not stand in the truth, because there is no truth in him. When he speaks a falsehood, he speaks what is natural to him, for he is a liar (himself) and the father of lies and of all that is false."*

SATAN LIES! HE LIES TO US ABOUT GOD —
HE LIES TO US ABOUT GOD'S LOVE *and* WORD!
Satan speaks what is natural to him ... he LIES ABOUT YOU!

The devil is the father of lies and of all that is false.
He's a murderer ... a Killer!

The devil is the Master Deceiver.

Jesus says, *"The thief (Satan) comes only in order to STEAL and KILL and DESTROY: I CAME that you may HAVE and ENJOY LIFE and HAVE it in ABUNDANCE (to the full, till it overflows)."*   John 10:10

Enemies kill! SATAN *IS* THE ENEMY! HE IS
THE DESTROYER, THE THIEF, THE KILLER,
of every thing good … of love, lives, minds, ministries,
marriages, finances,
emotions and health!

The Greek word translated *"destroyer"* means "ruiner; specifically, a venomous serpent." Satan is a destroyer, a "ruiner".

He came only to ruin; to STEAL, KILL, *and* DESTROY!

Then, Jesus came! Jesus came to give us His *"abundant life to have and to enjoy to the full, until it overflows!"*

Jesus came to love us extravagantly!

Jesus loves you! Jesus literally physically died for you! *And,* He spiritually died for you. Then He gloriously rose from the dead … FOR YOU! That's as extravagant a love as you can get!

Jesus comes only to protect, provide love *and* give us His abundant, full, and rich Life to have!

"Be well balanced (temperate, sober of mind), be vigilant and cautious at all times; for THE ENEMY of yours, THE DEVIL, roams around like a lion roaring (in fierce hunger) seeking who he MAY seize upon and devour."   1 Peter 5:8

The devil roams! He was kicked out of heaven. He was cast out! Cast down! He was made to leave Heaven! He was sent to earth! He roams the earth seeking people who will give him permission ... people who will allow him to seize them *and* devour them! God tells us to be *a-ware* ... not beware!

"But the (Holy) Spirit distinctly and expressly declares that in latter times some will turn away from the faith, giving attention to DELUDING and SEDUCING SPIRITS and doctrines that demons teach, through the hypocrisy and pretensions of liars whose consciences are seared (cauterized)."   1 Timothy 4:1, 2

Satan, through his demons, tries to teach! Some people listen and turn from their faith in Jesus to seducing spirits, and lies of the devils!

Satan wants to deceive us, knock us down, beat us up, and kill us!

And Jesus wants us to know, *"For the Son of Man did not come to destroy men's lives, but to save them (from the penalty of eternal death)."*   Luke 9:56

Jesus does *not* beat us up *or* break us down!

Jesus came *to* save us! He loves us!

Jesus did not come to beat us up and leave us crying, lying bleeding in a pool of lack, defeat, sickness, and despair!

The devil is wild. He roams the earth to lure you into biting on his tricky bait. He baits you like an animal! He tries to lure you *into* error! He seduces you into doubt, defeat, and despair! He wants you confused and away from Jesus, and His Word!

The devil wants to hook you and reel (mislead) you *away* from Father God's Word and His Love for you! And he'll try any way he's allowed! Once you're hooked, he'll cook you up to eat you alive! But, God's cookin' *and the* devil's well done!

Are you getting the picture here? Can you see what a filled with hate, destroying, murdering enemy you have?

Be encouraged! Do you see God's got you covered?

God sent His Son Jesus! He plainly tells us in John 10:10, *"… I CAME that you MAY HAVE and ENJOY life, and have it in ABUNDANCE (to the full, till it overflows)."* Jesus is an abundant giver! He gives us life to enjoy till it overflows! He does not destroy spirits, minds, bodies or lives!

JESUS WILLINGLY CAME!
HE WILLINGLY CAME and GAVE US His rich Faith Life!

His Life of Faith is our protective Life! We have His Life to enjoy in abundance. Now, on this earth, we can have the Faith life of Jesus to overflow in us! Glory to God! We can REJOICE that we have Jesus!   Romans 3:22-26; Galatians 2:16; 3:22, 26; Ephesians 2:7-9; 6:23; I Timothy 1:14; Hebrews 12:2

Look around! Can you see, SATAN ACCUSES, LURES, DECEIVES *and* DESTROYS LIVES, not God?

God's Word *in Jesus* saves! Jesus heals lives!

God's Love *and* Word exposes Satan for the destroyer that he is!
Isaiah 14:12-17; Revelation 12:7-11

The enemy is lying to you big time every time you're hooked into filling your mind with fear, doubt, or hate!

Satan wants you to doubt God's love for you! He wants you to doubt Jesus and His Word! The devil lives to hook you into fearing, being depressed or worried or anxious about your life!

You can resist the heckling devil by listening and praising God's love for you through His Son Jesus. Stand on God's promises that He loves you *and* provides for you. God will never leave you or forsake you! Your loving Father created you to receive His love! He will always richly protect you and provide for you.

SATAN DESIGNS LIES!

Remember, the devil can't do anything but lie! He is the father of lies; a murderer! He lies *about* God. He lies *about* you. He lies *to* you! All he speaks is false!   John 8:44

But, Child of God, you are protected! Praise God, for His love and protection! We can choose! We don't have to listen to or be deceived or depressed by the devil! We can choose our rich, loving LIFE in Jesus!

We have a choice, according to Deuteronomy 12:11, 18; 14:23; 30:19-20; and the book of John!

"I call heaven and earth to witness this day against you that I have set before you life and death, the blessings and the curses; therefore choose life, that you and your descendents may live and may love the Lord your God, obey His voice, and cling to Him. For He is your life and the length of your days ..."   Deuteronomy 30:19

Many of us have chosen curses over blessings ... we made wrong choices! And some of us have made a series of wrong choices! And these choices changed our lives forever. Just look at what wrong choices cost Ananias and his wife!

Peter said, *"... Ananias, why has Satan filled your heart that you should lie to and attempt to deceive the Holy Spirit, and should (in violation of your promise) withdraw secretly and appropriate to your own use part of the price from the sale of the land?"* Acts 5:3, 4

Satan lied to Ananias! Ananias listened! He was baited into lying. First, he chose to listen to the devil. Then, Ananias chose to look at his circumstances, listen, and act on what the enemy had said! And then Ananias chose to lie! He attempted to deceive the Holy Spirit! He chose death ... he made wrong choices and he fell down and died! The choice Ananias made cost him his life!

Satan offers you nothing but despair *and* death through his suggestions!

He always offers you a deception which leads to death and away from life in some form or fashion ... sometimes that deception is even clothed in a half-truth!

Then the enemy will suggest that you start talking and walking in his deception!

Remember, Jesus says, *"... the devil ... he was a murderer from the beginning and does not stand in the truth, because there is no truth in him. When he speaks a falsehood, he speaks what is natural to him, FOR HE IS A LIAR (himself) and THE FATHER OF LIES and OF ALL THAT IS FALSE."* John 8:44

Satan always speaks lies, falsehoods, *or* half-truths! He began with Eve in the garden when he asked her was she sure about what God had told her to do! He lied and baited (tempted) her into doubting God *and* His Word! Eve choose to listen to the enemy! Then she acted on his suggestions!

Genesis 3:1, 4, 5

Satan is the Tempter! He tempted Jesus, *"And he (Satan) said to Him, 'IF You are the Son of God, THROW Yourself down (from this temple tower); for it is written, He will give His angels charge over you, and they will bear you up on their hands, lest you strike your foot against a stone'."*

Matthew 4:6

Satan was lying! He quoted, but he perverted, God's Word from Psalms 91:11, 12, by suggesting to Jesus that He challenge God by throwing Himself off the tower. The devil twisted his lie further! He told Jesus to trust God to save Him on the way down, after He had thrown Himself off that temple tower! Satan was trying to use Jesus to boldly challenge God!

Has the devil ever tried to use you to boldly challenge God?

Jesus *knows* **His Father** *and* **He** *knows* *and* **He** *believes* **His Father's Word!**

Jesus knows all about His Father God's love for Him! Jesus wasn't about to fall into Satan's trap! Jesus knew that He loved His Father! He wasn't about to put His Father or heaven's angels to this deceiving test!

Jesus is confident! He *knows* He has the saving power, rich love and Word of His Father! Jesus *knows* Satan is the liar!

Jesus knew that the devil didn't *know* Father God's Word! Jesus knew the devil can only repeat what he reads or hears! And Jesus *knew* that the devil repeatedly uses, and misuses, and perverts Father's Word!

Jesus zeroed right in on him! Jesus called his evil lying hand big time. He boldly told Satan, *"The Scripture says, YOU shall NOT tempt the Lord YOUR God."*   Deuteronomy 6:16

The next time you are being tempted by the devil, boldly speak these same powerful words to him from the scriptures!

Wow!   Jesus chose to ignore the lies of the devil! He

chose to *speak* His Father's Word! Jesus knew, spoke and He trusted Father God's Word! He reminded the devil that His Father is God and Lord! Now that's choosing to speak life over death in confidence and authority. Jesus knew that He is Lord and God over the devil!   Matthew 4:7

Satan will make up, suggest and try to speak more lies and tales to you than you can keep up with! His every tale will be opposite to God's love for you!

The devil tries you every way he's allowed! He'll tell you,
     "You're not worth anything!"
     "How do you know you can trust God?"
     "HA, God's Word ...
          you know you can't BELIEVE that!"
     "You can't believe or trust in God!"
     "Well maybe you can trust God; but surely not other
          people, or especially yourself!"
     "Look, you'll never make it!"
     "You're not smart enough!"
     "Who do you think you are anyway?"
     "You're a nobody! You're a failure!"

"Look how many times you've failed!"   (a big lie)
"You know what you do won't work!"
"You know nobody really cares about you anyway!"
"Nobody really cares what you think!"
"You'll never amount to anything!"

You see, the devil, through his lies, attempts to deceive and destroy your joy and walk with Jesus ... by designing fear! He uses doubt, unbelief, confusion, anger, hate, *and* despair!

STOP! Doubt your doubts!

Or here's a big one the devil tries to put on you,
"God may not love you ... How can He love you!
"You don't love God!"
*" Look at how messed up you're thinking and feelings
are and how messed up you act!"*
"You're not good enough!"

Or, Satan suggests to you,
*"You know you can't understand God. He's a mystery,
complicated ... He's God!"*
"Just look at the mess your in!"
"God won't listen or speak to you!"
"God doesn't hear you! You're a loser!"
"You better not do (act on) God's Word!"
"What will people think?"
"You have prayed ... why hasn't God answered?"

OR, what about this big lie?
"You're not healed ... you still feel the pain!"

ALL *ARE NEGATIVE* BOLD FACE LIES OF THE
DEVIL HIMSELF. Lies conjured up from hell's pit to drive
you away from God's Word and from God's love! His lies are
designed to fool you and make you fear … then try to lead you
away from Jesus and into doubt, unbelief, anger, despair,
defeat, sickness, poverty!

A nd if these simple negative suggestions don't work
on you, then Satan will twist his own lies around
and suggest to you, just like he did to Ananias and Jesus,

> *"If you're the greatest; go ahead, God loves you … you can
> do ANYTHING! You are fear-less!"*
> *"You can do anything; jump off this temple tower!"*
> *"God will bless anything you do?"*

God will not (*can not*)
bless *anything* we do.

First, line up your thoughts and actions with God's Word!

Let's understand right here:

God is the Creator of Divine Order!

**This Universe operates efficiently in God's created
Divine Order of His Faith *and* Love!
God gave us His Perfect Son Jesus!
Jesus, God's Love in His Word … is His Divine Will!**

When we're trusting the Lord Jesus, lining ourselves up with His Love and Word for us … we're boldly walking in God's Divine Order!

In Jesus, we love and believe as we walk *in His Word*! *In Jesus*, what we say and do lines up with God's Word! *In Jesus*, nothing we say or do will be out of His will! God promises to honor His Word and He performs His own Word!

Deuteronomy 9:5; 1 Kings 6:12; Jeremiah 1:12; 29:10, 11

God's Word tells us to trust Him ...
    in Jesus we trust Him!
        God's Word tells us He loves us ...
            in Jesus we love Him, and we believe His love!

In Jesus, God's Word says He has thoughts of peace for us and He provides for us! We believe it! As we walk holding onto God's Word, *in Jesus,* we don't doubt.

Child of God, *expect* God to honor His own Word! He said He would! We believe and receive what God says is the truth! God is the truth! God does what He says! We can trust the integrity and excellence of God and His Word!

We can step out of un-belief and into *all*-belief with Jesus!

God tells us Satan set out to deceive, *"The coming of the lawless one (the antichrist) is through the activity and working of Satan and will be attended by great power and with all sorts of (pretended) miracles and signs and delusive marvels — (all of them) LYING WONDERS ..."*

2 Thessalonians 2:9

Satan deceives, with all sorts of *pretended* miracles!

Most of us have heard Satan's lying suggestions (words). All Satan does is with *lying wonders ...* only pretended!

Satan can *appear* to be positive and powerful! But the truth is, he is weak, deceptive and power-less! The coming Antichrist will even be escorted in by Satan's lying, pretended miracles, signs and lying wonders!

The devil can mix just enough of God's Truth with his lies, to make his lies *look* like the truth. **Enough so that he will fool an entire world of people!**

When I was a young teenage girl in the 50's, I was told, *"If you ever have sex with a boy, or get pregnant, you <u>have to</u> get married."* Now, that statement looked exactly right. But it doesn't suggest the loving way to Godly marriages and Godly commitments.

What those words say are, *"If you have sex and "mess up",* you <u>have to</u> get married, you <u>have to</u> get married, you <u>have to</u> get married." Some teens had sex and got pregnant just so they <u>had to</u> get married!*

Then, sometimes when you made a mistake you would hear old-time sayings like, *"You made your bed, now you have to lay in it!"* No forgiveness; no hope! What a tragedy!

Oftentimes these unloving, confusing messages forced many teens into guilt and to get married! They would marry to try and hide or to correct their mistake of having sex or getting pregnant outside of marriage.

At worst, in the 50's and 60's, a mother would give her baby away or have a secret abortion! Just like today, abortions were often the way out of fear! To hide and to avoid religious, family and social rejections … abortions began!

Should a so-called "marriage" not last and you divorced, you were again condemned and viewed as an outcast!

Can you see how harsh and cleverly twisted this thinking was outside of God's Word on forgiveness, godly love, marriage and intimacy?

Women were labeled as failures ... looked down on by most church goers; kicked out of the family; rejected by society. All these scenarios smacked of horror, ruined lives, total defeat, and lack of God's forgiveness, and certainly no love!

I heard and learned many of these dangerous, twisted, manipulating, unloving ways of thinking.

I heard many old sayings and traditional *marriage rules* play through my heart and head like a drum. And, on the surface, all sounded reasonable! But, Praise God, I have also learned none of it lines up with God's Word or His truth in His love for us on sex and marriage!

You see, "THE TRUTH" IS ALWAYS JESUS, and HIS LOVE! GOD is His Word ... *and Jesus and The Word are all Truth!"*
John 1

Marriage was never intended by God to be entered into only because of a social or religious manipulation or correction rule for sex. And sexual desire or need is not to be feared or entered into or used as a trapping tool! Sex has been perverted and used for centuries to hook people into ungodly relationships ... lifetime commitments of marriage ... to break up families, marriages and married partners! Look at David and Bathsheba!

God hates all lies and manipulations ... "bed-hopping" and divorce! But, adultery or divorce is a forgivable mistake, not an un-forgivable sin. In ignorance, we have all made mistakes.
Proverbs 6:16-19

In the love of Jesus, be forgiving and never condemn or reject anyone for their mistakes or their ignorance of the love of God ... or for their being involved in relationships that are perverted or doomed to break apart without God.

For Great success, put God's Word first in your life!
Psalms 1:1-3

God is abundant Love!

Jesus is forgiveness ... He is His loving Word!

Jesus is The Truth *and* Love!

Marriage is one part of loving God's beautiful plan and design for spiritual, mental, emotional and physical union in Him! It's His commitment between the married partners *and* Himself!

Marriage is intended to be a spiritual union ... a oneness!

Just as God's oneness is with Jesus ... as humanity we are united in spirit as One with Father God and Jesus. As believers, we are the Bride. Jesus is the Husband! He loves us! We love Him! Isaiah 54:5; John 3:16; 16:27; Romans 5:5; Revelations 21:2

Marriage is a beautiful spiritual and physical union which takes place within the heart of God! This unity occurs with God in the hearts of those married!

If before and during marriage, couples diligently studied God's Word and His beautiful truth of being connected to His heart in marriage ... there would be far more successful marriages and fewer divorces!

No doubt, when both partners put and keep God and His Word and love of Jesus first place in their individual lives *and* then in their relationships, marriages grow stronger and divorces decline.

As we learn God's love … as we receive His love, we begin to see the lies … *the* half-truths the devil has designed to destroy lives!

God's love is for us! In His Divine Order, He put marriage in place as one remarkable way for us to have honor for Him for ourselves, *and* for each other! God divinely planned for us to honor and glorify Him … within the married relationship.

And yes, Satan will try to tempt and bait us again and again to stray off! He wants us to go outside of God's Love and Divine Order … blundering around, making bigger and bigger mistakes and acting opposite to God's loving Word!

Jesus was tempted again! *"Again, the devil took Him up on a very high mountain and showed Him all the kingdoms of the world and the glory (the splendor, magnificence, preeminence, and excellence) of them."* Matthew 4:8

Still, the devil said, *"These things, all taken together, I will give You, if You will prostrate Yourself before me and do homage and worship me."* Matthew 4:9

Again, Satan lied to Jesus. Satan made Jesus a false, twisted promise!

Satan wants Jesus, *and you,* **to bow down to him!**

He offered to give Jesus the glory of kingdoms of this earth that he knew were not his to give! But, Jesus already knew that the kingdoms of the world didn't belong to the devil! Jesus knew that everything in the universe, every star and grain of sand, every kingdom already belongs to Himself and His Father ... *and all* belongs to us in our Inheritance with Jesus!

Just imagine the arrogance and pride of the devil to try and make a phony deal and tempt Jesus with what he knows doesn't belong to him! The devil knows better, yet, not only did he try to make Jesus a phony deal, he asked Jesus, ***"You bow down before me and worship me!"***

Satan is bold ... filled with hate, arrogance, and pride ! He wants his own evil power ... he wants to be *like* God! Pride (self-importance) was his downfall from the beginning. Remember, he even asked Jesus to bow down to worship him! And your evil enemy is still asking today.

The devil uses trickery, phony fear ... false pride! He will tell you, *"You aren't important!"* These become some of the devil's most nasty, wicked, and sneaky temptations.

Every time Satan tempts you or tries to bait you to fall into one of his deceiving traps, know that what he is really asking you *and* Jesus living inside you, is to bow down and worship him! It's not so hard to see the devil is our enemy, is it?

Satan, already knew that Jesus had powerfully overcome his temptation to jump from the temple tower ... potentially killing Himself! Yet, he still persisted! He still heckled Jesus with his twisted *false* promise that all the kingdoms of this world would be His *if* Jesus would bow down to worship him!

When Satan tempted Jesus, remember what Jesus told Satan to do? The same thing we can tell him to do!

"Then Jesus said to him, 'BEGONE (get lost) SATAN! For it has been written, YOU SHALL WORSHIP THE LORD YOUR GOD, and Him alone SHALL YOU SERVE.' Then the devil departed from Him, and behold, angels came and ministered to Him."   Matthew 4:10, 11

Jesus said, *"Get lost!" "It is written!"* Jesus always spoke His Father's Word over Satan <u>reminding</u> him again of God's Word as Lord over him!

Jesus knows and understands that He is Lord over Satan! Jesus knows that Satan has to bow down and worship and obey Him and Father God. Jesus knows that He's Lord on the Throne and He's not nervous!
Psalms 47:8; Matthew 5:34; Hebrews 1:8; Revelations 7:11-12, 15-17; 19:4; 22:1-4!

The Lord is on the Throne *and* He's not nervous!
Psalms 45:6

Child of God, *in Jesus*, you are One with Almighty God. Jesus lives inside you! You too can choose to speak God's Word over your circumstances and you too can speak God's Word and tell the devil to leave, *"get lost"* … and he will leave!

Jesus has given us all of Himself!
Stand up, praise God,
speak out Father God's powerful Word!
His Word is His truth!

Honey, the Lord Jesus is *alive and living* inside you! Do you understand that the Lord is on the Throne and Satan has to bow down, obey, and worship the living God living inside you?

Do you know that just like for Jesus, angels come and minister to you?

In two different temptations Jesus chose to *boldly* remind Satan that Father God is his (Satan's) Lord *and* his God. Jesus *told* the devil, *"YOU* (satan*) will bow down and worship and obey the Lord YOUR God!"*

Jesus boldly, powerfully reminded the devil that he (the devil) will absolutely bow down, worship, and obey God!

We too have this over-coming choice!

We can choose to live by God's abundant blessings of Love, provisions, protection and Word ... or ... we can choose to live by the curse's of Satan's lies, fears, temptations, doubts, and lack (have not)!   Deuteronomy 30:19, 20

The devil has been told and ordered by Jesus to obey and bow down to worship the Lord God, *and* serve Him! Satan must bow down! I must keep asking you, *"Do you understand that Father God is the Lord and God of Satan?"*

Should you ever hear Satan's deceiving, lying words ...

SPEAK UP!   LIFT YOUR VOICE!
**Remind the devil your sins are forgiven ...
remind him you're set free!
Tell the devil Who he's to obey!**
Isaiah 43:25, 26

JUST LIKE JESUS DID
Say Jesus' bold Words, *"GET LOST"*!

Tell Satan you know Who he has to obey and worship ... the Lord, his God.

Tell Satan, *"I obey God alone."* Tell Satan, *"I live by God's Word!"*

Press Jesus, the Living Thorn, into Satan's side!

Jesus, *in you,* is the Living Thorn in Satan's side!

Remind the devil
that he has to
obey *and* worship
the Lord God
just like he's supposed to!

Tell Satan to take his nasty hands off you because you're God's property! YOU BELONG TO FATHER GOD! Tell him he can't touch you! Tell him your spirit, body, mind, and heart all belong to God!

Stand firm on your Father's Word!

As you receive and act on the integrity of God's Word and keep focused on Jesus alive, living inside you ... you'll be amazed at the results. God is always with you. HE NEVER LEAVES YOU ALONE!

The devil carries a big magnifying glass! He uses it to magnify himself! He uses it to magnify himself and to try and make you think that he is bigger and more powerful than he is!

Satan tries to magnify your circumstances to look worse to you and bigger than they are! Of course, he wants you to think and talk about how big, how overwhelming your circumstances are!

Take Satan's big ole' magnifying glass he carries around, away from him!

God wants us to know, *and* speak His Love, His Truth, His Words!

Take his big ole' magnifying glass and turn it around! Then, *look* right through it into the protective, powerful, loving, Beautiful forgiving Eyes of Jesus!

If you're going to look at something, *stop looking* **at your circumstances ...** *start looking* **at your magnified Jesus, and** *look* **at your Victory of love** *in Jesus.*

Jesus is always looking! Jesus is always with you, loving, looking over every circumstance in your life.

Jesus knows just exactly what's going on in your life at all times.   John 6:64

1 John 3:19, 20, *"... we are of the Truth ... we can reassure our hearts in His presence ... Whenever our hearts in (tormenting) self-accusation make us feel guilty and condemn us. (For we are in God's hands.) For He is above and greater than our consciences (our hearts), and He knows (perceives and understands) everything (nothing is hidden from Him)."*

God is greater and He knows all about us, (nothing is hidden from Him, He sees and understands all) ... God sees beyond what we can physically see! *In Jesus ...* when we accept we are of the Truth, *we remain the Living Thorn* in Satan's side!

Let's remember, if how things *look* **(how** *we see* **things) don't line up with God's bountiful forgiving love and His Word for us ... then, how things look are** *truly not* **how it is!**

Do you see Jesus is The Truth? How we *see* things or what we think or feel, if it is opposite or contrary to Jesus, God's Word and Love ... it is not The Truth!

God tells me, *"Rose,* ***I LOVE YOU! I love all My Children!*** *I want you to understand you are anointed to go speak My Love and Word to the world! You can stand in My Love; walk in My Love! You can listen to (obey) Me! I want you to speak, act on, write, and publish My Love and Word for you! You are victorious in Me!"*
Matthew 24:14; Mark 16:15; Acts 10:38; 1 Corinthians 15:56

1 John 4:4, 5 assures us, ***"For whatever is born of God is victorious over the world; and this is the victory that conquers the world, even our faith. Who is it that is victorious over (that conquers) the world but he who believes that Jesus is the Son of God (who adheres to, trusts in, and relies on that fact)?"***

"Rose, My Son was unmercifully beaten, rejected, spit on, mocked, slapped, nails driven through his body to a wood cross ... hung to die ... killed! I sent Him to die, and to live again inside you ... for all the world ... for you ... I love you!"
Matthew 26:67; 27:30; Mark 10:34; 15:19

Can we even imagine the horror leading up to the death of Jesus? Can we even fathom the torture, the pain, the torment in the body, spirit, mind, and heart of our Lord?

Can the Great God, *"I AM"* deliver us from every circumstance in our life that is not of Him? You bet He can!

When you're talking to God, saying the Lord's prayer, *"... and lead (bring) me not into temptation, but deliver me from the evil one ..."* you are believing God's assurances that you can not be tempted by Satan beyond God's deliverance!

In the very NAME of Jesus, you are a danger to the enemy.

2000 years ago, you were personally delivered from all power of Satan *by Jesus.* You can believe Satan was forever paralyzed, defeated by Jesus ... he's not even able to come around you or talk to you unless you let him!

God operates in belief - *not* unbelief!
Put God's Word first *and* into action!
As we believe God, we can watch Him operate!

God tells us, *"Look to Me and be saved ... for I Am God and there is no other!*
The devil (and all his demons) in heaven, on earth and under the earth, every knee shall bow down to Me ... in the NAME, the powerful Name of Jesus ... and every tongue confess that Jesus Christ is Lord, to the glory of God the Father!" Isaiah 45:22, 23; Romans 14:11; Philippians 2:10, 11

The devil *knows* **he has to bow down** *and* **OBEY GOD'S WORD...!**

YES, Satan *knows* that he absolutely has to bow down and obey God's Word, *spoken* by you, in the NAME of JESUS, in His Authority! Your loving *Jesus is alive* living INSIDE YOU … the devil doesn't want you to know any of this "Good News"!   Romans 8:10, 11

YOU resist *and* discourage the devil *with* God's Love!

YOU speak God's Word *and* Praise Jesus to the world!

God's Love terrifies the devil!

Praise God's Authority and His Love Jesus living inside you!

When the enemy hears you praise God and speak God's Word over him, (in the Name of Jesus in His Authority) HE HUNKERS DOWN, BOWS DOWN and then RUNS fast, squawkin' like scared baby chicks!

Did you ever hear or see squawkin' scared chicks run?

Well, David and I live on a farm. And glory to God when baby chicks are scared they are going to be hurt, caught, or they sense danger, they bow so low to the ground and run so fast squawkin' to get away from you, you just nearly fall on the ground laughing.

You see, Satan runs faster than squawkin' scared chicks! He bows down to your authority IN CHRIST and love in Jesus. He hightails it squawkin' in fear when he hears you speak the very Name of Jesus!

God's Word and Love, coming from your heart and mouth, terrify the devil *and* remind him he's defeated!

Can you see why Satan wants you ignorant and doesn't want you to know or believe God's love ... or hear you speak God's Word?

God's loving Word exposes Satan *and* his lies!

Satan hates the very Name of Jesus! He hates the Truth and Authority of God that defeated him and has power over him!

Satan hates the Truth ... he hates THE Jesus that defeated him 2,000 years ago.

Satan dreads and fears Jesus (The Truth) ... because Jesus The Truth has exposed him for over 2000 years as the forever paralyzed, defeated, lying enemy that he is!
                    Colossians 2:15;   Hebrews 2:14; 1 John 3:8, 9

As you stand firm in God's word, the enemy is constantly reminded that Jesus is Lord ... over you, inside you, and over him! The devil is reminded Jesus is Lord all over him!

The very NAME of Jesus reminds Satan, the defeated enemy, that Jesus loves you.

Your boldness and love of Jesus reminds Satan that you are God's Beloved Child and that by the very Name of Jesus he is powerless!

JESUS IS YOUR:
LOVE
THE TRUTH
YOUR DEFENDER—YOUR DELIVERER!

If you're facing any problem today, don't try to handle it on your own.

Get with the Main Man Jesus! Speak the NAME of Jesus!

Praise the over-coming ability and love of Jesus living inside you! Child of God, *"You have the mind and love of Christ!"* 1 Corinthians 2:16; 13: 1-8

Boldly ask Jesus to raise up inside you with His loving, wise Mind, alive in you … in His Wisdom and knowledge, to help you solve your problem!

Yes! You have the Mind of Christ! You can think and act *in Jesus*! Praise Him! Thank Him!

Remember,
SATAN
IS THE defeated LIAR
and THE ACCUSER!

Jesus is your Defender — your Deliverer!

CHAPTER 2

JESUS IS
YOUR DEFENDER - YOUR DELIVERER
~
SATAN IS THE ACCUSER!

Revelation 12:10, *"And I heard a loud voice saying in heaven, Now is come salvation, and strength, and the kingdom of our God, and the power of His Christ: for the accuser of our brethren is cast down, which accused them before our God day and night."* (kjv)

Some people do not know that Satan works like a prosecuting attorney! The devil runs into the very Throne Room of God. He goes there to file charges against you. The devil speaks and falsely accuses you day and night before God! *If we let him,* he will destroy our lives, and he absolutely falsely accuses you to others! Satan is a slanderer ... The Accuser!

Satan criticizes and condemns! He condemns you before God! He wants you accused, guilty, prosecuted, executed ... put to death! Satan is a killer! He cares nothing about you! He wants you condemned and out of his way!

BUT, Saints of God, we have the Defender *and* Deliverer, *"So too the (Holy) Spirit comes to our aid and bears us up in our weakness ... He Who searches the hearts of men knows ... because THE SPIRIT INTERCEDES and pleads (before God) in behalf of the saints ..."* Romans 8:26-27

You see, Holy Child of God … as a saved saint, a believer (not a condemned saved sinner), the Holy Spirit (Jesus) stands with God for you! He is blessed to come to your aid and plead for you! The Holy Spirit of God defends you before Father God in your time of weakness … all on your behalf!

The Holy Spirit is sitting right there with Jesus in that heavenly courtroom! They are talking about you with Father God and coming to your aid in the Throne Room of Heaven!
John 20:17; Ephesians 4:8-10

Jesus is gladly your Defender—your Deliverer! He's your Protector! He's your defense attorney in heaven so to speak!
1 John 2:1

And who do you think God is listening to? Do you think He listens to the devil? No, no, no! God listens to Jesus, the Holy Spirit! He listens to YOU! Remember, He hears you! So what are you saying to God?

How you talk can cause your life to go up in smoke!
James 3:5, 6

Lots of people say, *"talk is cheap!"* **Not according to God!**

Just like on earth, if you were accused of a crime you needed acquitted from, or a crime you didn't commit, you have to give Jesus something to work with in order to defend (protect, safeguard) you. Let's take a closer look at how we talk and *how* important *what* we *say* is!

Death *and* Life are in the power of the tongue!
Proverbs 18:21

"By our words we are justified and acquitted and by our words we will be condemned and sentenced."   Matthew 12:37

When we talk about how sick we are or weak or poor or sinful we are or fearful or defeated we are ... we are condemning ourselves ... how can God work with that? If all we're able to speak about is how worried, scared, burned out, poor, tired, in lack or angry we are ... God can't operate in that!

God operates in faith! He *can* defend us as we faithfully, boldly praise Him, and speak (confess, talk) His love and victory over us. No one Jesus ever healed or delivered ever disagreed with Him about being set free! They believed Him, praised Him and followed Him ... even though they didn't know exactly Who He was!

God hears what we *say*!

If all Jesus hears is our talk of fear, struggle, sin, shame, and doubts ... how can He defend that?

Honey, Jesus already took from us every sin and possible evil and diabolical assault Satan can dream up! Jesus did away with all this in His death and resurrection for us! We are completely protected by Jesus! **Let's talk about it! Let's praise Jesus for all He has done for us!**

The devil hears what you say. Let him hear your abundant praises and faith in the Lord!

Jesus completed *all* for us! You see, the earth doesn't

belong to the devil. The devil just moved in! We let him take
over!   Psalms 24:1; 1 Corinthians 10:26

You know how the story goes! When you let an "unwanted
nasty" bully its way into your life ... you keep hoping that
"thing" will leave soon ... but soon doesn't come ... until *you*
make it come!

The tongue is a fire!
James 3:6

When I learned that God hears me and I realized that He
listens to me, I had to examine my mouth *and* my attitude. I had
to change what I was *saying*. I had to stop whining and crying!
I had to quit talking only out of my natural human reasoning.

I had to stop talking fear, worry, pity, defeat, sin, lack, and
despair! I had to start receiving God's forgiveness, forgiving
myself, and others!

I had to start talking about my Father's love, power,
abundant provisions, protection, forgiveness, and victory over me!

**Trust God!
He will
take care
of you!**

I had to start lining up my heart and
my mouth with God's Word! God's
Word says in Mark 11:23, 24 ... *"I can
have whatsoever I say!"*

Stop a minute and think about that!

Can we even consider how we sound to God?

When we disagree with or contradict God and humanly
reason or whine and cry or complain about life ... what is God
hearing from us?

Jesus said, *"I have come to give you life ... to enjoy ... I am the Good Shepherd!"*   John 3:16, 17; 10:10, 11

Jesus gave us abundant Life ... His Life ... over-flowing ... for us to enjoy! Let's abundantly talk about it!

1 Thessalonians 4:13, *"Now also we would not have you ignorant, brethren, about those who fall asleep (in death), that you may not grieve (for them) as the rest do who have no hope (beyond the grave)."*

Don't live as those who have no hope.

You're a believer!

God's Son Jesus shed His Blood to free us up and clean us up from all worry, despair, defeat, sickness, poverty and sin.

Jesus rose from the grave victoriously having defeated, for us, *every* evil thing of the devil for all eternity.

So, make up your mind right now to speak out *and* live like the victorious winner God made you to be and you'll spread the knowledge of victory in Christ everywhere you go!
                                   1 John 1:7

God's best is set on His Banquet table for you now ... so you can eat!

I can tell you, if even one of my children went out every day talking in fear, worry or doubt, crying and whining, telling the neighbors about how bad they are and how scared and worried they are ... and how they never know for sure that I love them or I will feed them, or let them sleep in their bed that I gave to them *and* belongs to them ... I would have to sit down to have a serious long talk with my unhappy, misinformed child!

With these kinds of statements I wouldn't have anything to defend them with, would I?

And then each morning, if my children woke up whining, complaining or came home at night and fell to the floor at my feet pleading with me to just give them a little sip of water and a tiny bite of white bread ... while I'm asking them to sit down to eat eggs, hot biscuits and gravy, or delicious golden fried chicken and warm buttery mashed potatoes sitting on the table right there in front of them ... why I would think they were blind! Or, maybe really ignorant ... or just plain disobedient!

Child of God, let's open our *spiritual eyes*:

God has set for us
His Kingdom size banquet table!

He has provided us with choice steak, eggs, hot biscuits *and* gravy, golden fried chicken *and* warm buttery mashed potatoes ... just for us!

Do you see how God thinks and desires to bless us? If we're not abundantly eating from His banquet table maybe it's because we can't find the table? Or, maybe we don't believe His kingdom table of abundance is there?

Or maybe we're too busy begging for scraps and leftovers to realize that God's table of abundance … His banquet … is set for us!

We pray and ask God to meet our needs! He says He has and will! So what can be wrong?

Prayer asks … Praise Him *and* receive!

According to Luke 22:29, 30, Father God has set for us His kingdom banquet table of abundance. Praise Him, pull up to His kingdom table and sit down—sit down and eat *with* Him!

Jesus says, *"… I give you the privilege to eat and drink at My table in My kingdom and sit on thrones …!"* Praise Him!

Every person on this planet earth can have Jesus and eat and drink at God's abundant kingdom banquet table! Let's start today … believe Him … sit down … and eat with Jesus!

We have *His* thrones to sit on and *His* Words to *speak* in our Father God's joy and abundant love for us! Let's *talk* about our abundant Jesus! As we speak about His extravagant rich love for us … we honor Jesus as our glorious Provider and our Deliverer.

Tell people Jesus is the "Good" Shepherd!

Let's pull up to God's kingdom banquet table of Love and over-flowing provision! Let's *talk* about His Great love and abundant provisions of joy, a sound mind, prosperity, health, and protection for us!

Let's praise Jesus! Let's *receive* and walk in His Great Love for us!

We can *stop* complaining and whining! We can *start* talking about how the earth is full of our Lord's goodness! GOD LISTENS to us! He hears every word, from every person on this earth! He hears our praises!　　Psalms 33:5; 111:4

God hears you! He wants you to hear Him!

- God wants us to hear ourselves! Stop the negative!
- He wants us to stop talking fear and doubt!
- Stop talking defeat and receive all His victory for you!
- God is your *loving* Father! Talk about it!
- What are you *saying* when you talk to Father God?
- Become God-conscious and stop being sin-conscious!
- Are you listening to the devil … and then speaking defeat, worry, begging, and whining and crying?

Or, are you listening to your Lord Jesus, receiving all His blessings, gifts and abundant rich love and provisions for you? Are you praising Jesus as your Defender and your Deliverer?

Or, are you talking about what a no good, rotten sinner you are? Is your head spinning as you talk about this sorry world?

Jesus said, *"I assure you, most solemnly I tell you, if anyone steadfastly believes in Me, HE WILL HIMSELF be able to do the things that I do; and he will do even GREATER things than these, because I GO to the Father."*　　John 14:12

Child of God … *you are* a believer:

1. You have the privilege *and* power of the living God.
2. He is alive inside you, helping you.
3. When you speak you know Father God is listening.
4. You have His ability to act … in the Name of Jesus.
5. You can do greater things than Jesus did.
6. Jesus says you're an over-comer … victorious!

To anyone, to everyone, *tell them that* Jesus is your Savior *and* your Lord *and* Good Shepherd, Defender—your Deliverer, and your abundant (more than enough) Provider and Love!

We can listen to (obey) Jesus! We can receive and do God's powerful Love and Word *through* Jesus! And because Jesus rose from the dead and is alive for you … inside you … you can not only do what He did, but He says you can do greater things than He did by telling people Who He is … your good Savior and Lord … THE Savior and Lord!

Read God's Word! Then speak God's Word! Tell people that you are who Jesus says you are in the Name of Jesus! Praise Jesus!

Go tell people Jesus is their Great Provider!
Psalms 65:9

Tell them, Jesus laid down His Life for them and He lives for them !

Tell them, God says they can trust in Jesus and depend on Him to defend them, deliver and abundantly provide for them!

Tell them, to tell somebody else so they can receive His freedom, His love, and *all* He has for them!

Psalms 23; John 10:11

With the Father, Jesus is *your Praise … your Savior, Lord and Good Shepherd!* He is with you to lead you! He is always with you to provide for you, help you, and guide you!

In Jesus, when we talk in His love we do even greater things than Jesus did by telling people all about what Jesus did for us! Tell people the Good News of Jesus! *Jesus loves* … He lives … He is All Good.

Talk about how Jesus is able to be their Savior and Lord …

Jesus is our Almighty Defender and abundant "Need Meeter", our protector, and all praise! Jesus is The Way *and* The Truth *and* The Life! You *know* Him! Turn God's goodness loose inside you and tell people!   John 14:1-7

Tell people Jesus loves them so much He died for them!

Tell people Jesus died *and* right now He lives … for them!

Tell them of His Love … death …Life … set them free!

Tell them, *in Jesus*, they are completely set free from struggle, fear, doubt, worry, sin, sickness, *and* disease!

Tell them!
Isaiah. 53:4, 5;   Ecclesiastes 2:26;
1 Corinthians 1:30; 2:16; James 1:5, 6

We *are* the anointed *by* God! We *have* His Wisdom to use!

Luke 4:18, 19, *"The Spirit of the Lord (is) upon Me, because He has anointed Me (the anointed One, the Messiah) to preach the good news (the Gospel) to the poor; He has sent Me to announce release to the captives and recovery of sight to the blind, to send forth as delivered those who are oppressed (who are downtrodden, bruised, crushed, and broken down by calamity), to proclaim the accepted and acceptable year of the Lord (the day when salvation and the free favors of God profusely abound."*

The Spirit of the Lord is available upon all of us! *In Jesus,* you and I are ordained and anointed [have been given God's Spiritual Authority and power (ability)] to announce freedom to the captives!

In Jesus, we are anointed ... given spiritual authority to give oppressed, broken down people His freedom through His love!

We have gigantic authority *in Jesus* to encourage people to listen to God! We can announce His freedom for us, the Good News of Jesus!

Child of God, *in Jesus*, you are especially chosen *to go* and send forth as delivered those who are broken down by calamity.

God's Words of His Son are for us to use, to proclaim His salvation to each other! We are to tell each other ... that His free favors profusely abound.

God says, we are anointed with His Authority to preach (speak) this Good News of His healing abundant love in the freedom of Jesus!

Jesus tells us, *"Behold! I HAVE GIVEN YOU AUTHORITY and POWER TO TRAMPLE upon serpents and scorpions, and (physical and mental strength and ability) OVER ALL THE POWER THAT THE ENEMY (possesses); and NOTHING shall in any way harm you."* Luke 10:19, 20

WOW! Read those scriptures again ... out loud ... slowly! Can you see these powerful scriptures taking hold of the richness of abilities we have from God in Jesus?

He says, *"I have given you authority and power to trample over all the power of the enemy ... <u>nothing</u> in any way shall harm you."*

Great News! GOD's cookin' *and* *the* devil's well done!

What is God's power? His glorious love Jesus and His Word are His power! Do we speak His power and authority over every situation in our lives? If not, let's speak His word out and operate in His love, mercy, grace ... His anointing and authority!

We rejoice in Jesus, we have the anointing (sacred appointment) of Father God's precious Love! We have Jesus!
1 John 2:27

With Jesus, we *have* the anointing of His spiritual, physical and mental strength ... His power! We *have* His knowledge, His wisdom ... His Mind to use! We *"have His Mind, we no longer live in the flesh, but to the will of God"!* We rejoice in His Love that our names are written in heaven!
1 Corinthians 2:16; 1 Peter 4:1, 2

In Jesus, beloved, we *have* the anointing, the Spirit of God's Power, His Will, in His authority, to stomp down the enemy. We *have* Jesus!

By Jesus, we have the powerful loving Word of Jesus alive on the inside of us!

With Jesus, we are completely God equipped *and* God protected from all harm! Psalms 91 says so!

Through Jesus, we have all God's Love, His Word, and His Authority to speak over the enemy!

You might be thinking,
>   *"Well Rose, if I have all this power why am I so*
>   *bound up and miserable?"*
>   *"Why can't I quit smoking?"*
>   *"Why can't I lose weight?"*
>   *"Why can't I quit drugs or alcohol, or going in and*
>   *out of bad relationships?"*
>   *"Why am I fearful, angry, and hurt?"*
>   *"Why am I so worried, depressed and tired?"*
>   *"Why do I stay in such a financial mess?"*
>   *"Why am I so sick and my health is so bad?"*
>   *"Why do I keep going from one crisis to another?"*
>   *"If God's Word is true, why is there so much misery?"*

… Because you're speaking defeat! You've let Satan convince you to look at circumstances and look at him, instead of speaking, and looking to God's Word and Jesus.

Do you realize that *you* can't change any of these things? Listen! Do you realize that God can and has changed all of these things?

Remember, ***"<u>nothing</u> in any way shall harm you …!"***

But, *you can stop talking* about how miserable your world (the world) is! You're *talking fear and doubt* about why and what *you* can or can't do! **Stop! Listen to what you're saying!**

The devil has you thinking and speaking that you are under his authority of the things you want changed. Or he has you thinking *you* alone have to stop or quit something *you* can't!

The enemy has you talking and thinking that you are under his authority in your circumstances.

You may be speaking or listening to many negative words like, *"look out ... you can't, you won't, you haven't, you didn't, shouldn't, couldn't, wouldn't ... you better not!"*

But remember, *"... **with God all things are possible!"***
Matthew 19:26

Are you constantly hearing all about how *you* can't do anything about circumstances in your life because *you* never have?

In the Kentucky mountains we say, *"Bologny, hogwash!"*

This is great news! Now that you know *you* can't whatever, God can take over, and with your cooperation He'll work that thing out.

In God's Word ... *His* Work ... *His* Love ... *in Jesus* ... our living Christ, we have all the authority and power we will ever need ... *to get the job done!* We have His Love, His grace, forgiveness, mercy ... His peace!

I bet I have lost and gained 10,000 pounds in my life. Up and down, down and up! I even said once, *"I've given God my fat!"* Guess what, God doesn't want my fat and He doesn't need it.

Then, I found out I needed to *quit talking* struggle and defeat! I needed to speak God's victorious Word over my circumstances ... I didn't need to give God my fat or pray to lose weight.

Read Romans 12:1 and 1 Corinthians 6:19 and say, ***"I present my body to God as the temple of the Holy Ghost, which dwells inside me ... for I am not my own ...!"***

What I needed was delivered!

I asked God to deliver me from an overwhelming desire for more food than my body needed! I began to praise Father God!

Do you see what I'm talking about?

Wrong *thinking* equals wrong *talk* equals wrong *actions* equals wrong *results*!

Now that I'm *listening* to God, speaking His Word over this area … I've quit thinking about food as my joy. I've quit looking for and thinking about food as my joy every minute of the day! I am treating my body and feeding my body correctly.

Jesus is my joy!   Not food!

I now eat good food to live instead of living to eat. And for an Italian country lady, in ministry, that's pretty radical. Now I live to eat God's good food—His Word, *and* good foods for my body!

Which way did God create our spirits, bodies, and minds? Does God want our minds and hearts over-flowing with worry and anger? Does He want our bodies or lives over-flowing with only candy, pastas or cake?

Does God want our minds and spirits fed with worldly junk? Or does He want our whole being, spirit, body, and mind, filled correctly … filled, with His spiritual and physical foods … correctly eaten in His love?

> **God created us to hunger for Him!**
>
> **The world is starving for Jesus!**
> John 6:35

God wants us filled in His thoughts … from His Words!

Our spiritual needs and our physical food needs are all important to God! Sometimes our spiritual hunger needs get mixed up! Our spirits hunger and are starving for Jesus … then we start eating physical food to feed our starving spirits and emotions!

Worry and food can become twin gods!

Physical food can be a god! Or, we can go the opposite direction and starve ourselves and not properly take care of our bodies! Then we pig out and act like we did it all right.

Stop talking worry, doubt, lack *and* misery over yourself *and* other people!

We need to learn to consistently *and* persistently in the Name of Jesus, lay our head on the lap of our precious Jesus *and* rest!

We must learn to *quench our thirst by speaking* God's Words of love, in balance and care over our spirits (hearts), bodies, our minds!

Jesus is our food … our thirst quencher!

We can safely, correctly, and consistently feed our whole person! We can learn how to feed and love ourselves the way God loves us. *Through Jesus,* God abundantly feeds us! Father God heals our bodies and renews our minds with His Word ability!

God gives us His Word ability! God expects us to get His understanding on how to treat ourselves, and others. He wants us to treat ourselves and others, the same way we want to be treated ... **the same way He treats us.**   Matthew 7:12

God's Word has plenty to say about how we are to talk, feed, and treat ourselves!

Jesus says His consistent abundant love, Word *and* care for us *is* His food!
Deuteronomy 8:3;   Matthew 4:4

God has plenty to say about our correctly eating physical food and diligently, consistently eating, and living on His *spiritual* food ... His Word!

People are hungry! People are starving for Jesus! Sometimes people try to fill their hungry hearts and bodies in all sorts of harmful ways ... foods, drugs, sex, money, shopping, excessive work, careers, religious rules, unhealthy relationships!

Romans 12:2, *"Do not be conformed to this world (this age), (fashioned after and adapted to its external, superficial customs). But be transformed (changed) by the (entire) renewal of your mind (by its new ideals and its new attitude). So that you may prove (for yourselves) what is the good and acceptable and perfect will of God, even the thing which is good and acceptable and perfect (in His sight for you)."*

When we feed and apply God's Word to our hearts over each area of our lives, *He renews our minds with His Word! He* transforms our thinking ... He changes our lives ... He fills to the brim ... to over-flow and fulfills every physical, spiritual, and mental hunger we have ...!

Jesus said in Matthew 4:3, *"... we live not by bread alone but by every Word from the mouth of God ..."* By speaking and walking in His Word, God's Word renews ... transforms our mind! We then start to live and rest in His Love!

God knows we are starving for Jesus! He created us to live ... to really live! He created us to have this hunger and desire for Jesus! Glory to God ... God gives us His hunger!

WE HAVE GOD'S WORD and LOVE to feast on! I can't say enough about feasting on God's Word ... and being filled with Jesus! Jesus fills us! He sets us free from every earthly hunger as we feast on and speak His Love!

Often, due to ignorance ... in a lack of *receiving and knowing* God's Love, the world struggles to the point of physical starvation, despair, and death.

We have the credible love of Jesus and God's Word to receive. We have His Love for us to speak *and* use. Most people don't know they have it. They just keep on struggling and talking all about their sickness, fears, worry, sin, lack, and misery.

Let's even go a little further. *"Then why does the following happen, Rose?" Reverend Kenneth Hagin speaks of this event ...*

"Suddenly, the phone rings. The voice at the other end screams, *"Turn on the news, turn on the news."*

The news flashes from scene to scene. The newscaster's voice reels with emotion:

"A family of four, found murdered and robbed today. Traveling from their home, Pastor Al Jones, his wife and two children were kidnapped and mercilessly killed by an apparent robber who murdered all four, then stole their vehicle. Details at 11:00 tonight."

Viewers are shaken! The inevitable question is asked. This same question will be asked — over and over ... *Why did this horrible thing happen to them? They were wonderful people; a good Christian family."*

The answer to this question could be harder to believe than the murder itself. In this life, we may never know the truth of their death for sure.

Most people will try, without success, to help God out with the answer. What looks like a desperate tragedy screams with people's opinions based on religious ideas and traditions.

It could be years before important information is discovered. Information that no one talked about at the time because they thought it was unimportant.

Perhaps someone remembers hearing this family repeatedly saying and talking about how, *"they always believed they would die a tragic death together!"*

Father God is not a beast, a killer, or responsible for horrible tragedies!

Do you hear those words?

Then, statements are made like,
"Well, God knows what's best."
"You know the Bible says, 'All things work together for good to those that love God ...'!"
"The Lord giveth and the Lord taketh away."

Foolish words and statements are spoken and God is made out to look like a beast, a killer; or at least that He is responsible for these horrible deaths and other tragedies.

Please pray! Let the Lord lead you to see the power that God says words have!

God needs to stop being made out to look like He is roaming the earth snatching people off of it with death and tragedy.

Let's stand in what God says in Proverbs 18:21, ***"Death and life are in the power of the tongue: and they who indulge in it shall eat the fruit of it (for death or life)."***

Yes, *"Death and life are in the power of the tongue ... !"*

You speak what you believe!
2 Corinthians 4:13

Negative or positive!
You will get what you say!

Let the weak say, *"I am strong!"*
Joel 3:10

Jesus tells us, *"We will account for our every word!"* Matthew 12:36, 37

The tongue and what comes out of the mouth is very important to our Father. He speaks about it over 142 times throughout the Word.

What kind of attitude and words are coming from our mouths?

Are we speaking God's Words ... His Good Life ... His love, His victory over ourselves, our circumstances and others?

Or are we speaking what I call the five D's ... doubt, defeat, despair, destruction, and death?

Are we speaking deadly words of fear, despair, worry, sin and sickness?

Are we spewing out of our mouths idle tales and nonsense words ... little jokes and snippets we say are harmless?

" ... *Out of the abundance of the heart the mouth speaks!"*   Matthew 12:34

Let's examine our hearts and words today! Let's read God's Word ... let's fill our hearts to speak all His Life words that God wants us to say.

Let's get radical about how we talk.

Can we make a decision today to change our gossip words, our anger words, our fear words, our condemning or critical or un-forgiving words ... our words of misery, doubt, lack, and struggle ... our "laugh it off" words?

Can we stop chit chatting, complaining, or condemning?

If need be, let's change our defeated words into His victory Words! Let's use our Lord's life giving, victorious Words ... filled with His knowledge of His abundance and wisdom!

Your mind is a word bag ... a storage container!

Empty out
your negative word bag!

If need be,
clean house in your mouth …!

Fill up, pack full, your word bag, your mind container, your heart, your mouth, with God's positive abundant words of praise, glory, appreciation, gratitude, joy, love, peace, strength … then,

God says, *"let the weak say I am strong!"* Joel 3:10 *"let the poor say I am rich because of what the Lord has done for me!"*

Remember God's Banquet table? His table is set with His choice steak, eggs, hot gravy, hot biscuits, delicious golden fried chicken, warm buttery mashed potatoes, hot apple pie, and sweet vanilla ice cream.

Let's praise God from our mouths and watch Him use all He's provided in His faith Words … His life giving words … His faith force … to work wonders on our behalf!

Is God the killer … the destroyer?

Is God walking the earth robbing and taking people off of it with starvation, disease, death, despair, and tragedy?

What does the Bible really say?

Read God's "goodness" list!

JESUS IS YOUR:

- *LIFE*
- *REDEEMER*
- *LOVE*
- *FORGIVENESS*
- *HOPE*
- *FAITHFUL*
- *ABUNDANTLY GOOD*
- *PEACE*
- *JOY*
- *MERCY*
- *GRACE*
- *ABUNDANT PROVIDER*
- *PROTECTOR*
- *THE HEALER*
- *Your DEFENDER and*
- *DELIVERER*

The "goodness" list of Jesus is longer
than this book can contain!

God is *not* a killer! He gave us Life … His Life — Jesus!

We can receive God's best *and* we can rest in Jesus!

God is faithful! He says so!
Romans 3:3; 1 Corinthians 1:9; 10:13; Galatians 2:20;
Ephesians 2:10; 6:23; 1 Timothy 1:2; Titus 1:4

**SATAN IS THE SLANDERER … THE ACCUSER!
SATAN IS THE DESTROYER!**

The devil is our enemy … the Beast … a thief who comes to *try* and steal, kill, and destroy our joy, peace, faith, and love of Jesus!

Remember, the enemy will slander us, accuse us with our own words from our very own mouths.

The devil will use our own words, our own talk, to kill us … *if we allow him that opportunity!*

Satan is the sneaky thief!

Speak only God's Words!

Reach down into the depths of the heart of God and settle once and for all that:

Jesus is your love … your loving abundant "Need Meeter"!

CHAPTER 3

JESUS IS THE
"NEED MEETER"
~
SATAN IS SNEAKY
(the beguiling, cunning, seducing)
SUBTLE THIEF!
2 Corinthians 11:3

Honey, don't you let the devil put one over on you! He's the seducing, lying, subtle thief! Stay *a-ware*! You don't have to *be-ware*! Keep giving all glory to God that we have the victory of Jesus. We have His whole simple Truth to live in!

In Jesus, we know we're the victorious winners right now!

Matthew 6:8, 32, 33, *"... for your Father KNOWS WHAT YOU NEED BEFORE you ask Him ... for the heathen wish for and crave and diligently seek all these things (food, clothes, shelter), and your heavenly Father KNOWS WELL THAT YOU NEED them all ... BUT SEEK (aim at and strive after) first of all HIS KINGDOM and HIS RIGHTEOUSNESS (His way of doing and being right), and then ALL these things taken together WILL BE GIVEN YOU ..."*

WOW! Father knows what we need *before* we ask!

He promises us that He is our abundant "NEED MEETER"! How much more can Father God love us? He gave us ALL! He gave us Jesus! He gives us victories!

Every need you or I could ever have ... Father God already knows about. Father God *has* already met our every need *in Jesus*!

And He did this for us through the death, and life again rising, of His Son Jesus our Living Christ! Jesus is alive ... He is our *living* "Need Meeter"! Satan is the deadly "need thief"!

Have you ever watched a magic show? I know you realize that as you looked and you know you saw that magician open up his four inch flat, square briefcase and lift that huge 10 lb. round bowling ball right out of that flat little briefcase ... that it really didn't happen? And even though you think you saw it, you do know a bouquet of flowers doesn't turn into a cute, white fuzzy rabbit? You do know that your eyes, your mind ... that magician fooled you?

Just like that magician, the devil can make circumstances appear and look to you completely different ... or worse than they really are.

Honey, coins *don't* come out of ears!

Yes, you can trust and rely on God's Word to the extent that when Satan shows you something in the natural world that appears to contradict God's Word, you just say, *"Well, I saw that, but I'm not going to be gullible enough to believe it. I'm going to stick with God's Word on this!"*

God says, we can totally rely on Jesus now!

God says our needs are already met! God says that what He says *and* what He does is the truth!

Beautiful Child of God, **we can depend on Jesus!** We know that Jesus meets our needs!

1 John 4:18 says that we know we have His love! We can praise Him as our abundant "Need Meeter" for all eternity and mankind!

"And I will do (I Myself will grant) whatever you ask in My Name (as presenting all that I AM), so that the Father may be glorified and extolled in (through) the Son.
(Yes) I will grant (I Myself will do for you) whatever you shall ask in My Name."   John 14:13, 14

Jesus says, *"whatsoever you ask believing in My Name"*, Father always answers! Jesus tells us to seek, to knock, to ask (demand) in His Name!

Jesus *always* desires to give to us *and* to extravagantly love us *and* to richly provide for us … according to His Word!

Jesus came to give to us all we ask; not take away from us all He's given us!

As believers, we already have all of Jesus … we have all of His provisions and giving Love!

WHEN WE ASK *and* KNOCK He hears us! HIS DOOR IS ALWAYS, ALWAYS OPENED!   Matthew 7:7, 8, 11

He says we have faith because we hear Him, *"Faith comes by hearing (what is told), and what is heard comes by the preaching (of the message that came from the lips) of Christ (the Messiah Himself)."*   Romans 10:17, 18

Once we hear God's Word, then we decide if we will *believe* His Word! Then we decide to *receive* His Word! And finally we decide to *act on* (live in) His Word that we receive!

Faith comes by hearing and says,
"we know we have Jesus"!

We don't seek what we know we already have!

We live by faith in what we have!

Our part in seeking is to aim at *and* strive toward His way of doing and being right!

We can know we have *all* in Jesus!

Brag on Jesus! We can walk in all we have in His love, ability, His faith and Word with the authority of Jesus living inside us.

We receive Him and walk *living* in His total love and Word for us! We walk *in* faith … *by* faith … not by sight!

Faith comes by hearing God's Word!
Romans 10:17

"We walk by faith and not by sight"!
2 Corinthians 5:7

We walk by His faith in us … not by what we see! God knows us! **God has faith** *in* **us!** He has faith enough *in us* to love us!

God gave us *all* <u>His Faith</u> when He gave us Jesus!

We have all His faith we need, to believe, receive, and act on (live in) every Word of our Father's total protection and abundant provisions for us. Faith is a powerful spiritual force!

Remember, as we hear God's Word, we will decide if we are going to believe *and* receive what He says or not! *"Faith comes by hearing and hearing by the Word of God!"*

First, we hear God's Word!

As we hear, then we believe! Then we decide to listen to (obey) *and* receive God's Word.

As we believe, we receive. As we *speak* God's Word and begin to act on it (live in it), we can watch God's Word work! Look at how His divine order and process works?

First, we
   hear, or read, our Father's Word ...

Then, we
   believe ...

Next, we
   receive ...
   speak ...

Then,   *action takes place (we praise Him)!*

Ａnd all of His Divine ability comes from Father's faith, love, peace, and grace joined in our hearts.
Ephesians 6:23, 24

God's grace and His peaceful love is Jesus in our hearts! Jesus is our source! He's greater than anything in all this earth; this universe! Let's stay tapped into our greater power source!

1 John 4:2-13, *"Greater is He that is in you than he that is in this world … God sent His only Son so that we might have life through Him!"*

Jesus is in us! His grace is in us! His Greater Love and faith is in us! He gives us life and enables us to give (speak, teach, publish, act on) His Greater Word!

When we are loving and giving, we are releasing the power of the Greater, believing, receiving and giving … Great Jesus!

In the power of God's love WE ALL CHOOSE TO BELIEVE JESUS IS OUR ABUNDANT LOVE - GIVER … OUR GREAT ABUNDANT PROTECTOR *and* PROVIDER!

Or, outside of the power of God's love, we make the choice, without His love, to listen to the devil and to look out only for ourselves!

**You see, without love,
there is no hope … there is nothing!
And opposite to all that God is …
is the devil!**
1 Thessalonians 1:3, 4, 5

Satan is the "NEED" THIEF ... *If we let him* he will rob us of God's faith, hope, love, and Word! He will kill our desires and our needs! Satan's greatest suggestion to us is to FEAR ... then to doubt! He wants us to fear and doubt, think that we don't need, that we shouldn't have, and we can't love or be loved!

Satan's suggestive, destroying lying words sound like,
> *"You may not make it!"*
> *"Are you sure? Maybe you should just give up!"*
> *"You really don't want to give ... do you?"*
> *" What's love got to do with it anyway?"*
> *"You really don't believe you can do that, do you?"*
> *"Are you sure you're good enough to deserve that?"*
> *"How can God love you?" "You're not holy enough!"*
> *"But, what if ... what if what you're doing doesn't work!"*
> *"Are you sure God hears you?"*
> *"You really don't need that do you?"*
> *"Are you sure you can really trust God on this?"*
> *"God may meet your needs but He may not always meet your desires (wants)!"*

You see, Satan speaks his lies to cause you to fear and doubt! Then, he can steal from you!

Every thing Satan speaks are his attempts to hurt God ... to lead you into fear, loss, despair ... to pull you in the *opposite* **direction of the Word of God ... to lure you from the love, blessings and provisions of Jesus ... to lead you to destruction** *and* **potential death!** *Don't listen!*

Stop! *Take a minute to enjoy Jesus and, read, read, read out loud His Words in* Psalms 21:2–7; 37:4, 5; 91; *and 103!*

1 Thessalonians 5:8, 9, *"... put on the breastplate of faith and love and for a helmet the hope of salvation. For God has not appointed us to (incur His) wrath (He did not select us to condemn us), but (that we might) obtain (His) salvation through our Lord Jesus Christ (the Messiah)."*

Philippians 4:19, *"And my God will liberally supply (fill to the full) your every need according to His riches in glory in Christ Jesus."*

But, Satan tells you, *"Your doomed ... God won't help you this time, you can't, you couldn't, you shouldn't have and you better not!"*

The demon "buddie" devils of Satan will tell you,
"You don't need to give ... don't give ... you can't give or, you can't have, you better not ... God's gonna get you for sure on this one!"

"You already know Jesus all you need to know Him!"

"You're not worth anything ... especially in the shape you're in!"

Satan is a fellowship and a relationship killer! He tries to mis-lead you into NOT spending time with Jesus! He'll tell you to trust only yourself and not trust God!

STOP! *Listen* to the wisdom of your perfect Jesus living inside you!

**See how Satan strives,
he lives ... to get your eyes onto yourself,
onto your circumstances,
and off Jesus ... to rob you ...**

to use your attitude *and* mouth ...
he'll even use your mouth to curse God
if you let him!

Through his deceiving suggestions of fear, doubt, and unbelief, Satan tries to corrupt *and* steal your abundance, your peace, your joy, your faith, your love, and your wholehearted devotion to Christ.

When we listen to the devil, then speak and act on what he says, he absolutely steals *and* destroys our faith, our peace, our laughter, our love, our hope, our joy ... our health and even our very lives!

He tries to destroy our business', our jobs, our marriages, families, our children, our relationships, our lives! Are you missing peace and joy in your life?

Are you smiling less and crying more? Are you listening to Jesus or are you helping the devil harm you?

God created you to have His abundance ...
His total peace *and* joy!

Jesus came for you to have Him and enjoy Him ... enjoy your life, your loved ones, your work ... your ministry!

If we let the devil, he will destroy our health, our minds, our ministries, our intelligence, our creativity, our church, our business', our finances! The devil is the destroyer ... the Killer!

Again, do you understand God created us to love and be loved? We are to receive Jesus ... to have and walk in His Divine Health, Divine mind, a prosperous ministry, godly marriages, abundant finances, His re-created Divine life ... all to have to abundantly enjoy *and* to use for His glory!

Satan will always, always *try* to deprive *and* destroy every thing and every one of God!

As an example, you can see if we let the enemy have our thinking, then next will be our words, our actions, our relationships and marriages! The devil *tries to steal thoughts,* health, finances, and minds. The enemy feeds you words of fear or despair.

I know many people who actually think and believe they can't even have good food or a bed or a good place to live … much less an abundant godly life!

Often, these people are called hopeless or "homeless"!

You don't have to fall to fear or lack and despair! In fact, in Jesus, you shall never fall! 2 Peter 1:10, *"Brethren, give diligence to make your calling and election sure: for if you do these things, you shall never fall."*

> **We** *have* **the un-limited power** (ability) **of God!**

Do what things? What keeps us on our feet?

Diligence! Diligence!

Diligence to exercise your faith; to develop mountain moving faith!   1 Peter 1:1-10

Diligence to hear God's Word!
Diligence to walk in mountain moving faith!
Diligence to speak out, shout God's Words of victory!
Diligence to act on His Word!

You can't live a life of victory without diligence!

We have thousands of churches and ministries all over the world filled with born-again believers who don't exercise their faith enough to keep their heart or their head clear! And some wouldn't recognize faith if they saw it coming down the street with a red suit on! I can say this because I use to be one!

Rejoice! Rejoice! Praise the Lord! We have God's Word to listen to and not the devil! We can be *diligent* by giving ourselves more to God's Word than ever before.

Child of God, *you have the Mind of Christ*! You have Jesus living inside you to listen to ... let yourself abundantly live and abundantly laugh in God's Word!

1 Corinthians 2:16; Philippians 2:5

March 1974, I *received* my glorious salvation of Magnificent Jesus. I thank God everyday, in Christ, that today I know I am a victorious Child of God! I now know we can walk with Jesus, and we can run victoriously with Him living inside us full-time!

Looking back, for as long as I can remember, Satan never stops! He never stops trying to stop us from *knowing God, knowing* God's Word, and *doing* God's Word. It is the devil's nature, his job 24 hours a day ... to try and deceive us, to make us think we will fall! It is the job of the devil to bring dishonor to God!

The devil does not want me, or you, to know or act on or live in faith in God's Love! He does not want us to know we *have* the faith of God, or that we can give God's Love and Word, with Jesus, to this hurting world!

GOOD NEWS! 24 hours a day, Jesus never stops enjoying us, loving us *and* providing us His faith *and* power to protect us!

We are equipped *to love, give, forgive, and* to *resist* the enemy!

In faith, *in Jesus,* we are submitted to God!

Early on, in my past ignorance of God's love and Word for me, I remember thinking I was weak ... powerless! I fearfully gave Satan permission to wreck my health ... steal my finances, my joy of Jesus, my peace ... relationships, ministry, marriage ... my joy of life, and the joy of my loved ones!

We *are* equipped to submit *and* resist!

Even in my early ignorance, as a believer *in Jesus*, God's grace gave me victory over death, cancer, hepatitis, an eye disease that blinded me, grief in the early sudden death of my loved father, divorce, food, financial losses, worry, defeat, un-forgiveness, strife, bitterness, resentment, confusion, poverty, depression, anxiety, fear, stress, anger, hate, doubt, and distress!

And these just name a few of the enemies deadliest offers!

One day, I read these powerful staggering words in 1 Corinthians 15:34, *"Awake (from your drunken stupor and return) to sober sense and your right minds, and sin no more. For some of you have not the knowledge of God (you are utterly and willfully and disgracefully ignorant, and continue to be so, lacking the sense of God's presence and all true knowledge of Him). I say this to your shame."*

"Utterly and willfully disgracefully ignorant ... lacking the sense of God's presence and true knowledge of Him!"

Talk about gloriously ripping open a oozing scabby sore ... driving a sharp stake into the pitiful spiritual aching heart! Those are some powerful strong words of God's truth! I praise God He tells us, as His Children, if need be, to wake up, and return to Him!

I don't know about you, but once upon a time, this scripture fit me like a custom made coat! I had little idea of the magnitude of God's love for me *and* for all His children! Read that scripture over, out loud again!

Does anything in it apply to you?

In 1991, following a very difficult divorce ... I was a spiritual, mentally sick and tired, fearful, doubtful, emotional, worried, angry, ignorant ... a bitter wounded wreck!

I was ignorant of *and* I ignored God's extravagant Love and Word for me! When someone tried to talk to me, my heart was dead asleep ... I wasn't right minded! I had allowed myself to become a completely defeated and spiritually ship-wrecked, sinking boat!

Have you ever been willfully, disgracefully *ignorant* of the love and heart of God?

Let's take a quick look at that word *ignorant*!

Ignorant: lacking knowledge
in the dark
oblivious
unaware, unknowing
failing to understand
baffled, clueless
all at sea

Have you ever walked clueless … willful, unaware, in disgraceful ignorance of the love of Jesus?

In my past, in ignorance, I handed over to Satan my health, finances, relationships *and* years of joy, and peace in the Lord!

Stop ignoring God's Love *and* His Word!

For years, in ignorance, I feared, doubted, and argued with the Lord! I battled with myself, loved ones, God *and* Satan! I woke up every day in ignorance, shame and guilt … ready to go to war and to battle an already paralyzed, defeated enemy!

I ignored God's Love and His loving Word that says, *"Rest in Me! Rest in My Love!"* Read Psalms 37:7, 8, 9; Isaiah 30:15; Matthew 11:28, 29; Hebrews 3:18; 4:1, 6, 7 10, 11, 12.

"Be still and rest in the Lord; wait for Him and patiently lean yourself upon Him; fret not yourself … cease from anger and forsake wrath; fret not yourself … those who wait and hope and look for the Lord shall inherit the earth!"

Every day and night, I laid down to fear! I didn't want to be fearful. But, I *thought* I had to fight just to stay alive!

I repeatedly listened to the devil's lies and deceptions! I ignorantly, viciously fought already defeated devils! I battled with myself, God, my family, other people.

I listened to and acted on Satan's screaming lies! I would not listen to the gentle victorious, saving voice of Jesus!

I struggled ... I suffered every day in deep pain. I leaned on my own understanding. I ignored God's rest, peace and love of Jesus! And Proverbs 3:5 plainly tells us, *"Lean on, trust in, and be confident in the Lord with all your heart and mind and do not rely on your own insight or understanding."*

According to God's Word in I Corinthians 15 we can truly lack sense. We can completely lack the sense and trust of God's love and presence. We can be looking at our own understanding, our own hurts, and our own selves!

Oh yes, we can talk about God's love, preach about Jesus ... but when a storm blows in ... we whimper in fear, run off in all directions like a whirlwind, crying out the Name of Jesus while forgetting and doubting Him all at the same time. Talk about confusion!

We can ignore all knowledge of God's *un-limited* love for us.

I use to listen, in ignorance, to the thief, the killer, the robber! I constantly cried out and struggled! I walked holding hands with Satan, the very enemy I fought.

I spent years fearful of God, myself, the devil, and man. I *constantly* reacted, according to Satan's words of fear and lies. I became filled with fear ... I was fear-full!

I even carried a loaded gun! I feared for my life and the lives of my children! Can you imagine?

I grew more fearful of the devil and man than I was trusting of God!

You see, I refused, I neglected to *listen* to what God's Word said to me. I retreated *from* God! I *chose* to talk *and* walk in fear and doubt!

In willful ignorance of God's love and Word for me I repeatedly gave in to fear! Then, anger and hate! I bought into Satan's lies. Every circumstance I encountered became the biggest thing in my life. I served every circumstance as an over-whelming problem! I prided myself in being a great problem solver!

I became a full-blown adulterer. Ministry, people, work, fear, doubt and worry, anger and despair, just to name a few, became my gods and lovers! I served fear and worry.

But, you see, at some time or another, we can change our thinking. We can all learn that God is in control of our circumstances. Jesus alone is the Master problem solver!
Romans 14:11

Circumstances change when we stop listening to wrong voices and switch from wrong to right thinking.

"We listen to wrong voices *and* we make wrong choices."

"Wrong choices bring wrong results!"

I have listened to plenty of wrong voices and yes I made many wrong choices!

Many times, I listened only to *my painful, hurting* thoughts, and the frantic voice of my fearful, worried feelings!

I listened to direct threats, condemnation, voices of ungodly men! I listened to doubts, fears, and lies instead of God's Word or His Voice of Mercy and His Grace! I *talked fear!* I lived every day in utter fear and defeat! I did not listen to the power or Love of my sweet Jesus!

I had a bad self-image. In my heart I led a hopeless, defeated life.

I am not beating myself up here. I have some Good News for you!

One day, Jesus became the biggest thing *in* my life … not the circumstances *of* life … I learned that in Isaiah 53 and Matthew 8:17 that **Jesus set me free!**

I am telling you *in Jesus* **… I know you can move from fear, utter despair, and defeat … to total victory!**

God doesn't think you have a bad self-image!

Isaiah 55:7 hit me straight in the heart, *"Let the wicked forsake his way and the unrighteous man his thoughts; and let him return to the Lord … for He will multiply to him His abundant pardon."*

Jesus died to pardon us! He shed His blood and now He lives to make intercession for us … to be our Mediator, our active Intercessor … our defense attorney, in heaven, so to speak.

Jesus longs for us to know we have His righteousness to rely on. He keeps us in right standing with our Father.

The Lord wants to *multiply* His abundant pardon to us!

In the darkest of hours and storms of my life as I wandered in a dark foggy wilderness, I finally learned ... that no matter what, I am to continually and confidently praise and magnify the Lord. I learned that I needed to listen to Jesus and return to the Lord in these three things:

1. We are not alone. We have the Word (God's thoughts). We have the Holy Spirit to strengthen us! We have the mind of Christ.

2. We must draw close to people who are full of faith. Instead of reliving a problem, let them do the talking. **Make yourself listen.** Join in with their faith and resist darkness. God multiplies His abundant pardon to us.

3. Praise God! Do whatever it takes to make yourself praise. When we begin to praise, God's presence will turn back all worried thoughts and make them fall!

The mere fact that today you are reading this book, will read other victorious books of love God is giving me, and there is MERCY HOUSE / ROSE LEIBUNDGUTH MINISTRIES is a beautiful, powerful testimony of the power of Jesus. I am a walking confirmation that God's unbeatable plan(s) are for us to succeed and be victorious! *"He will multiply to you His abundant pardon." You see, God has great plans for you! Plans for your good and not your harm!* Look at Jeremiah 29:11-14; Isaiah 14:24, 25-27; 45:11; and Romans 9:17.

Jesus is victorious! You are victorious! He always loves and waits, asking us to stop and turn back to Him, to sin no more!

Jesus longs for us to believe Him ... to trust Him! He deeply desires to richly bless us!

If you want to read about someone who had a bad self-image and it still didn't keep him from success ... read about Moses in Exodus. He lived in the wilderness 40 years herding somebody else's sheep. Moses had lost all hope of the dream he once had of being the deliverer of God's people from Egypt.

But God didn't think so!

In fact, God came to Moses right where he was, in the wilderness. God didn't ask Moses about his shady, slippery past. He didn't even mention or require his credentials or ordination papers.

God told Moses to go to Pharaoh and tell him to let His people go Well, you remember the rest of the story. But, before Moses would go, he began to question God.

He said, *"Who am I that I should go to Pharaoh?"*

God heard Moses! God's response to Moses' question was, *"Absolutely, I will be with you!"* Exodus 3:11, 12. *Read those powerful Words again out loud!* Can you see how God stays focused on us and focused on His own Word for us?

It's easy to understand Moses. As we plunder and wander in our wilderness, we think and do most of what we do according to our fears or what *we,* or Satan, or *somebody* else thinks, instead of what God thinks or wants!

You see, at one time I feared failure *and* I feared success!

When God says for us to fear Him, He means *to respect, to trust* **Him!**

I feared and worshipped, obeyed and served, a ministry, talents and a man! I worshipped people ... I feared people ... I was *fear-full* of God. I was *fear-full* of His Love and Word! I did *my* best!

I worshipped man and God's ministry work instead of worshipping God. Can you see how dangerously extreme and backwards that was?

Father God asks us to fear Him, but, what he means is for us to have *"respect"* **for Him!**

God never intended for us to be *"fear-full"* **of Him or anybody!**

In my early years as a Christian I lived day and night on a speeding merry-go-round of fear and struggle! My heart literally cried out to God to help me ... but then, I would close my ears because I was *fear-full* of God and *fear-full* of what God might say or do to me!

I was terrified ... deceived! I was ignorant, unwilling, unable to believe God's Love and Word is good! I repeatedly listened to and followed the convincing suggestions, threats and lies of Satan and men. Instead of seeking God's Word, oftentimes I chose to listen to men and to others! I listened to the devil through others.

My heart exploded from pain and fear every day. I wrote volumes of journals and two sincere books attempting to rid me of desperate *thoughts* and *feelings* of despair.

Let's don't be surprised at how persistent the devil can be!

Recognize ... God says it's the devil's nature, his 24 hour work ... his mission to deceive, to rob, kill and destroy God's love and Word!   2 Samuel 14:17; Psalms 52:3-5; John 8:44

God's Grace never lets go!

As I became more and more unwilling to trust God ... I became more terrified to even look for the Jesus I so desperately needed.

Still, God never let go of me.

Then one day, by God's mercy ... by God's grace, I stopped the battle and turned! I stopped listening to wrong voices! I started listening to right voices!

God's grace gives you rivers of revelation.

I praise God His grace never let's go! Finally one day, after battling, allowing myself to be driven into deep hopelessness and trampled by giants of lies, fear, and doubt ... I read, I learned!

I learned in 1 Samuel 17, just as David *with* the Lord God's grace with him as he stood up to Goliath ... I told the devil, *"I will no longer be driven into deep utter despair ... fearing, giving you everything, even my life!*
Now you devil, get lost, and just stand back and watch the Lord in me!"

David's words to Goliath the giant became mine, *"I come to you in the Name of the Lord of hosts ... in this day will the Lord deliver you into my hand, for the battle is the Lords!"*
1 Samuel 17:45, 47

You see, the Lord God *is* our Deliverer! I had cried out to every thing and every one else to help me … then, by God's grace I began to stand with God in Jesus … Oh, to be privileged to listen to Jesus …

Oh, to hear Jesus tell us Who He is and what He wants us to do … Oh, to listen to Jesus and *know* Him in the most personal, intimate way possible.

> **It is the heart desire of God to reveal Himself to you!**

In the precious Name of Jesus, I bring you powerful, loving Jesus, the Lord God Almighty …

> **Come unto Me, all who labor *and* are heavy-laden *and* I will refresh your souls!**
> Matthew 11:28

One day, I clearly remember talking, *and* listening to the Lord! As I was studying His Word, Jesus ever so gently said, *"Rose, don't you want to know the person Who died for you … Who lives for you … Who asks you to give all your life to Him? Don't you want to know Me?"*

I stopped and said, *"Jesus!"* "In five lifetimes there isn't any way to ever learn the Bible? There is no way I can ever read all of this Bible and learn everything in it!"

Then I asked Jesus, *"You ask me to trust You! Yes! I want to* ***know*** *You!"*

I cried out ... *"Jesus, I want to know Who You are. Oh Lord, show me! Help me! I want to trust You. Lord, help my fears, doubts ...* <u>help my unbelief</u>*!"*

As easily as I can audibly hear anyone speak to me I heard God's Voice say deep within my spirit, ***"Rose, I am glad to hear that you know that you don't*** know ***Me. Now you can come to Me; you can rely on Me and learn of Me. My Word is Divinely revealed by Me into your spirit. I reveal Myself and My Word to you! I reveal Myself as I choose and as you ask Me. You do not know yet that I love you so much ... I love you enough to have died for you and to live for you! You will learn Who I AM! You will learn Whose you are, in Me!"***

Oh how God's loving Words of His comfort, provision, peace, His joy and love flow like deep rivers from a fresh Spring rain.

There is an awesome peace that fills us as we walk refreshed in His Divine Love and Revelation Words of freedom to all of us!

Yes, to know we *have* His perfect peace that we all want, need and hear about! To *know* that we *have His peace* that passes all understanding! His joy fills my heart every day! And all of this comes by coming to Jesus. He asks us to come to Him. Read out loud and see Him in Matthew 11:28.

Beautiful Child of God, His perfect Word ... His peaceful assurances are there for *every one* of us!

In every circumstance in our lives like faithful Abraham, Moses, Joseph, David, Peter, John, Mary Magdalene, we can know we have the Greater Jesus! We have the shed Blood Covenant of Jesus … **We have Mighty God's loving Word in charge of us!**

God *is* in charge of us! His loving Word totally accomplishes His Purpose for all of us!   Isaiah 55:11-13

Jesus *is* Lord and He *is* Love over this entire universe … not just this earth! Let's understand, God's sure Word from the beginning to the end is written in 37 books of the Bible from Genesis 2:4 through Psalms 12:6, 7 to Matthew 11:25 and into Revelation 1:8! Throughout all the Universe … **JESUS IS LORD! JESUS IS LOVE!** Jesus is the Almighty! **Jesus is in charge! The Lord God is the Beginning *and* the End!**

"I am the Alpha and the Omega, the Beginning and the End, says the Lord God, He Who is and Who was and Who is to come, the Almighty (the Ruler of All)."   Revelation 1:8

Go to the Main Man Jesus! Live, resting in His power! Rest in His Perfect peace and love. He is Ruler of this Universe.

Jesus gives us the desire to *listen* to Him!

Go to *and* stick *with* the Main Man
Who refreshes your soul!

As we *listen*, we can hear and believe our Father's Word … as we *listen, we hear* and we receive God's power, Love, Mercy, and Grace drawing us to Him.

Oh to learn just how much Father God draws us with His Son's shed Covenant Blood! He created us! Jesus draws us to stop, to take time to listen to Him … to be with Him!

Isn't it time for all of us to get off Satan's speeding merry-go-round? Let's get off his jerky roller coaster ride of defeat and despair, and quit struggling?

Jesus tells us to turn to Him! He tells us to sin no more.

As God's Children, the sin Jesus speaks about is the sin we all commit of not trusting, resting … listening to Jesus or believing Him!

> While we are **doubtful** *and* **unbelieving we are not trusting Him!**
> While we are condemning others we are not trusting Him!
> While we are condemning ourselves we are condemning others … and we are not trusting Him! STOP!

Jesus loves you! God, by His Grace, shows us how to stop! You too can stop! Turn to Jesus … take time for Jesus, and listen!

Father asks us to stop and listen to Him! He asks us to believe that Jesus is our Deliverer! *In Jesus*, we can no longer be intimidated by the appearance of *any* giant. We *are forever* delivered by THE DELIVERER!

Father God created us to *know* we have Him, His Word and His Love! Jesus came for us to *see* Him and our Father; to *know* Him … to *trust* Him!   2 Samuel 22

David in 2 Samuel 22:2 and 20, *"… The Lord is my Rock (of escape from Saul) and my Fortress (in the wilderness) and my Deliverer … He brought me forth into a large place: He delivered me because He delighted in me."*

Yes, Jesus our Lord is our Deliverer and He delivers us because He delights in us!

God knows,
the devil has many strategies!

Satan tries to come at us, appearing gigantic, dressed up, disguised in the cloak of old giant past circumstances ... old fears and schemes, just like old counterfeit money! And if old strategies don't work, the devil's fast to make-up his new counterfeit fakes to try on you.

Don't try to keep up on your own! The best way to recognize the devil's strategies (lies, fakes) is to *know* the Real Jesus! You *know* that Jesus is Lord, His Word ... your Love ... a Rock ... your Provider ... your Deliverer ... the Truth!

**When you *know* the real
it's easy to recognize
the fake!**

**You *know* the real ... Jesus!
You *know* the fake ... Satan!**

**You can stand
successfully against
the devil's strategies!**

**But before you do
you're going to have to make
these three decisions.**

1. **You must make the Word of God your final authority in every area of your life. Line up your thoughts and your talk with whatever God's Word says. God's Words are His thoughts!**

2. **You must decide and begin to live your life by faith in what God has said and says to you. The Bible says, *"Faith comes by hearing, and hearing by the Word of God."***

3. **Finally, you must decide to live not only by faith, but by the love of God because faith works by love. Without love, your faith won't work.**

Faith is the initial act of obedience. Without the Word, you can't have faith. Obedience is the only visible possible evidence that in our heart we believe God.

You can't make one of these decisions without the others.

Make all three decisions together and stand on Ephesians 4:27, *"Leave no room or foothold for the devil — give no opportunity to him."*

2 Corinthians 10:3-5, *"Cast out thoughts that challenge the Word and bring into captivity every thought to the obedience of Christ!" Stop right now* and read out loud all of 2 Samuel 22; 1 Peter 1:22; 2 Corinthians 9:13; 10:5!

Be obedient to Jesus! Give Father God all your thanks as your abundant Provider and Deliverer that He is!

Remember, at one time, I didn't *know* Jesus, I only knew *about* Jesus!

I asked Father, *"God, how can this be? I'm supposed to be a "good" Christian, I accepted Jesus as my Savior years ago?"*

Good without God is a zero!

On my own, I thought, *"I did good work! I was a good Christian!"* But, I ignored God's love! Proverbs 4:20, 22, *"attend to My Words ... for they are life and healing ... !"*

When we *attend, make a priority,* (consent and submit) to God's Word, we are loving Jesus as Lord, Provider, *Good* Shepherd, *and* Deliverer! Oh what a deliverance and victory we have from our natural fleshy selves, and the world when we walk with Jesus! *You see, as believers,* we are *in Jesus!*

Jesus is your Savior, Lord, Provider, your Good Shepherd, your Healer ... your Deliverer!

Yes! God's Word teaches us Jesus is Love alive! He is Love living inside us, drawing us, leading us ... walking with us! Jesus tells us, *"you know Me and I want you to give Me to the world!"*

Some people live a so-called good Christian life ... without really *knowing* God's Love or His Word. When you try to be good without God ... you get a zero!

Jesus said, *"You wander out of the way ... because you know not the scriptures or the power of God!"*   Mark 12:24

Non-stop, all day, Jesus makes His Word and grace available!

God gives us the desire
to listen to Him ... to *know* Him!

Jesus *speaks* to us
through His scriptures!

Let's praise our Lord Jesus that He pulls us away from fear, despair, anger, bitterness, un-forgiveness, and defeat ... He pulls us from the very doors to the pit of hell!

Let's praise Jesus as He teaches us how to walk in His Spirit in *His* goodness! Jesus helps us understand that He is our Lord of forgiveness and freedom! Jesus is forgiving, not condemning or judging or waiting to criticize us. God loves us!

Romans 8:1

God forgives us! We are already forgiven!

In Jesus, we receive our forgiveness. God gives us the hunger, desire, and longing to keep hearing about how much He loves us! Jesus will always want us to know that He extravagantly loves us!

In the awesome love of Jesus, I can boldly tell you,
*"You can deeply **know** Jesus ... Jesus will teach you,*
show you, help you to know Who He is!"
*"You **have** Jesus! You **have** His Love!"*
*"You can **stand** confidently in His love!"*
*"You can **walk** in His Spirit!"*
*"You can **live richly,** abundantly successful in your*
*Lord Jesus, His love and Word! You can **attend***
*to His Word! You can **meditate** on His Word"*
*"You can **trust** Jesus and **depend** on Him!"*
"You are His joy ... Jesus lives for you!"
"You are a Beloved Child of God!"

Matthew 9:28, 30; John 3; 14:7

Child of God, Jesus Christ is living inside you! Do you know and understand you are who Jesus says you are in Him?
2 Corinthians 13:5

Jesus thinks you're terrific!

How many of us have ignored Jesus and ignored His Love and allowed the devil to deceive us?

Has the devil not nearly destroyed us, or our loved ones, while we are ignoring Jesus? Satan is forever reminded, as God's love and Word grows in us that we know Jesus and we know the devil as the defeated enemy.

Beloved of God, you *are* in God's circle of His Love!

GOD'S LOVE GOD'S LOVE GOD'S LOVE GOD'S LOVE

your name

Father God's grace, His love for us, circles around our lives!

In God's grace, in the circle of His Love, right now today, release, give up ... let go of ... empty all the hurtful times of your past to be gone forever! Fill your heart with His love for you!

Satan is reminded every day that God wipes away every tear from our eyes!

Our former old conditions and order of things have passed away. Praise God, Jesus makes all things new!
Ezekiel 11:19, 20; Ephesians 4:23, 24; Revelation 21:3-7

God's Great Lordship Love
circles around us!

God protects us … in Jesus, we know His Great Lordship Love in our hearts.

If there ever was a time when you and I *must know* God's will and purpose for our lives, it is now.

In Jesus today, we are anointed to *know all things! We have His anointing. We have* Him as Great Lord! We are anointed to *know* His Great Word! We *know* His Great, merciful, forgiveness, His giving Love for us and for all mankind! **We have insight to perceive Him better! We are in Him!** *In Jesus,* **we can** *receive* **and** *give* **His love!**

1 John 2:20-25; 5:20

Every time we pray and worship our Lord God, giving His love to each other or loving Him and ourselves … the enemy is reminded of his eternal defeat … he is reminded of our eternal victory in Jesus!

Just one Word from Father God CHANGES YOUR LIFE FOREVER! One Word like Victory, or His words of love coming from His Word can change everything forever! Jesus as Lord gives you courage … Great abundant Life and hope to your heart.

Go back, *write your name inside* **God's big circle of love for you! Now, do you see God's Love surrounding you!**

God created us to share with Him in His circle of Great Victories!

God created us to share in His glory for us!

God *created us* to *know*
His Extravagant Love for us!

God did not create us to be failures or to fall!

We are in the compressed time of God changing and rearranging things, lining them up for His end time move of the Spirit.

The devil lives every day, planning, greater than ever, to *try* to kill you! He wants to rob you of Jesus' Love and Faith; to rob you of your faith! Satan knows his end is near! In fact, the devil has gone wilder than ever! He knows Jesus is love! He knows his time is short! And the devil knows you are God's child and he knows if you know who you are or not!   Acts 19:15

Satan *tries* to rob you of your *knowing* God's Faith in you!

The enemy wants to try to deceive us, provoke us, beat us down … beat us up. He does not want you to *know* God's perfect plans for your life or how to carry them out in His power. Satan is a killer! But, no matter how wild the devil gets, you're no match for him. Remember, you are God's holy child!

Satan lives planning to kill and hate! He plans to rob you of your love for Jesus and your love for others! It's his aim! He lies about Jesus; he hates and fears the very Name of Jesus!

Satan hates Jesus!

Satan has hated Jesus
from the very beginning!

Wherever Satan sees an opening to achieve his robbery and dirty work he'll *try* to harm you in order to hurt Jesus!

Satan wants to prevent *or* steal your knowledge of your faith in God! And, he lives to keep you removed from *and* ignorant of God's Word! He wants you … in the dark … fearful, angry, depressed, worn out, fed-up, and tired.

Honey, the devil wants you confused.

With no mercy, the devil wants you thinking your health, your finances, your circumstances, your entire life is hopeless.

Or, the enemy wants you to think you are able to do anything and everything on your own without God's Word or Jesus! Do you recognize any circumstances in your life where Satan tries to use you and abuse you? *If you let him,* he'll deceive you to hurt yourself, others, and jab hard at God's heart!

Satan tries (makes every attempt) to seduce, reduce, corrupt and rob you from Father's Word and your sincere devotion to Christ!

The devil comes to convince you that you have no hope! Or, to make you think that even *without* Jesus, you're the greatest!

CHILD OF GOD, you are a believer! *In Jesus,* you are the greatest! When Jesus died, you died with Him … as He is alive … so are you alive in Him! You are One with Jesus! Jesus *in* you *is* in full Authority over Satan! *"Even so consider yourselves also dead to sin and your relation to it broken, but alive to God (living in unbroken fellowship with Him) in Christ Jesus."*   Romans 6:3-10, 11, 12-14

God's heart dream
is our
fellowship with Him!

Stand on God's Word!

Colossians 1:12-13 is one of God's most freeing scriptures, *"Giving thanks to the Father, Who has qualified and made us fit to share the portion which is the inheritance of the saints (God's holy people) in the Light. (The Father) has delivered and drawn us to Himself out of the control and the dominion of darkness and has transferred us into the kingdom of the Son of His love, in Whom we have our redemption through His blood, (which means) the forgiveness of our sins."*

Let the enemy steal no more!

Read this scripture again! Thank the Father! Confess this scripture for yourself! Receive all the love, deliverance, and forgiveness God has for you from the enemy and your sins!

Read and confess your creator God's thoughts as your abundant Deliverer, Provider ... your plan maker, your abundant "Need Meeter" ... your Redeemer ... your praise!

Then stand on Hebrews 10:23, *"... seize and hold fast the profession of our faith without wavering; for He is faithful to His Word that promised."*

Honey, seize, hold fast to Jesus. You trust your love Jesus ... He *is* faithful to you and He *is* faithful to His Word!

Stand strong in Jesus, your Father God's Love! Act courageously on Jesus as the awesome "Need Meeter," Provider and Lover of you that He is!

Jesus praises you! He longs for your fellowship with Him! He desires for you to know all about Him!

You can trust Him, and praise Him for all you are *in Him*, and for Who He is inside you!

Jesus longs for you to *know* that you *know, that you know, that you know ... that* He is ALL for you! He is ALL for you that He says He is!

Child of God, Jesus *is* your Savior, Lord, Love, Good Shepherd *and* Deliverer!

He wants for you to attend (make a priority) to His Word and love.

As His Beloved Child, you can *attend* to His words. You can reach for your Bible and open to Proverbs 4:20-24, *"My son, attend to My words; incline thine ear unto my sayings. Let them not depart from thine eyes; keep them in the midst of thine heart. For they are life unto those that find them, and health (healing) (Hebrew: medicine) to all their flesh."* (kjv)

Attend: to give something top priority. To set aside other things so you can focus on it. *"ATTEND to My Words!"*

Proverbs 3:5-6, *"Lean on, trust in, and be confident in the Lord with all your heart and mind, and do not rely on your own insight or understanding. In all your ways know, recognize, and acknowledge Him, and He will direct and make straight and plain your paths."*

These two scriptures alone have enough of God's wisdom and power to rely on for every circumstance in our lives!

And if you haven't received Jesus as your personal Lord and Savior, then you can do so right now!

Turn right now to page 167 of this book and pray your prayer of salvation!

Pray, talk with your Lord Jesus Who loves you! Pray His prayer of salvation and receive Jesus in your heart!

Then, let me know by writing to me so I can stand and rejoice and begin to be in prayer with you!

Jesus longs for you *to know Him!*
He longs for you to **know that**
you are His Beloved!

You are who God says you are!

You are **His forgiven,**
delivered, healed and made whole, perfect,
protected, abundantly provided for,
Beloved Child!

ARE YOU BEING HECKLED?

SATAN IS THE HECKLER!

Jesus is your Praise!

JESUS PRAISES YOU!

CHAPTER 4

JESUS IS YOUR PRAISE
~
SATAN IS THE "HECKLER"

"Bless (affectionately, gratefully, praise) the Lord, O my soul, and forget not [one of] all His benefits—Who forgives [every one of] all your iniquities (evil qualities), Who heals [each one of] all your diseases, Who redeems your life from the pit and corruption, Who beautifies, dignifies, and crowns you with loving-kindness and tender mercy; Who satisfies your mouth [your necessity and desire at your personal age and situation] with good so that your youth, renewed, is like the eagle's [strong, overcoming, soaring]!" Psalms 103:2-5

Beautiful Child of God, Jesus Christ, the Lord God Almighty, is your praise! Move into the quiet waters of Victory with Him!

Jesus praises you! Forget not one of all His benefits!

Jesus your Lord:
RENEWS YOU
- **Forgives**   • **Dignifies**
- **Heals**   • **Crowns**
- **Redeems**   • **Satisfies**
            • **Beautifies**

Bless the Lord! **You are renewed in Jesus!** Jesus satisfies your mouth *(your necessity and desire at your personal age and situation)* with good *so that* your youth, renewed, is like the eagle's *(strong, overcoming, soaring)*!

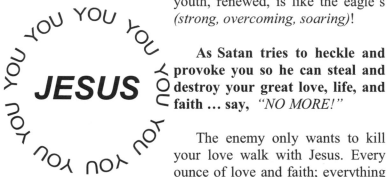

As Satan tries to heckle and provoke you so he can steal and destroy your great love, life, and faith ... say, *"NO MORE!"*

The enemy only wants to kill your love walk with Jesus. Every ounce of love and faith; everything good that God ever wanted and created you to have and be ... Satan wants to rob right out from under your nose! The devil wants you to feel weak, powerless, and useless! The devil wants to kill your praise!

But, Satan is a defeated foe!

Stay Christ-centered!

Colossians 3

We cannot compromise with philosophy or with legalism or with religious ideas, or with racial, gender, social, or economic ideas ... all are man-centered!

Child of God, Jesus is your center! He is your real Life! The devil can not harm you when you are Christ-centered! Hold on to Jesus!

Love drove Jesus to die and rise again for you so you could have Him! *In Jesus*, you have *all* God's protection, provision ... His love and victories!

Live in Jesus' enormous, extravagant rich love for you.

When the devil tries to get you to move, tell the devil you did move! YOU tell him you no longer live on his "Defeat Street"!

Tell the devil you live at 777 Glory Rd, in "Victory Kingdom" … with Jesus! Let him know you don't ride his bus any longer.

You don't have to give the "heckler" devil one inch, one second in your life! If you sense him trying to creep into your "Victory Kingdom", YOU SAY, *"Keep on movin' devil, cause I'm not ridin' on your bus again!"*
Matthew 16:23; Mark 4:15; Luke 22:3, 4

YES, God's Love and Word tells us we abundantly have Jesus' total love and Power! We have the Authority of Jesus and His Word to live in! **Kick the devil in the head with God's Word!**

In Jesus you stand, walk, and run courageously in God's authority of His love! Begin today to practice walking in God's Authority, in His Word, His love, and His powerful Name!

Take back all the "heckler" devil ever talked you out of!

HOW?

Tell your loved ones you love them. Show them every day, more than you already do, how important they are to you! Be forgiving … loving … giving!

Reach into the depths of your heart and generously reach out to give Jesus more than ever before!
Give to those you know are hurting! Give to those in

need! Pray for those in ministry who feed you spiritually … then give to them as unto the Lord!

Begin today, in whatever *circumstance you're in,* to abundantly give and trust God! Look up God's Words of authority over every circumstance in your life!

Then begin, in His peace and Love, to confidently and boldly speak the Word of God over every circumstance in your life!

When you speak God's Word confidently and boldly in His love Satan can't tell the difference between you and Jesus ! He thinks he is listening to Jesus!

In Jesus' Name, in your faith and the Great Faith of God living inside you, Satan thinks he is listening to Jesus! This sends him running.

JESUS *IS* YOUR LOVE! I cannot emphasize enough here about *knowing you can act … on* Jesus … as your LOVE!

Stand on, hold onto, hang with, wrap yourself up in God's loving blanket of Psalms 91:7, 10 and believe that *"God is your Refuge"* … *"a thousand shall fall at your side, and ten thousand at your right hand; but no evil shall come near your dwelling or befall you."*

Believing in Him is *knowing* Him! Trusting in Him is *knowing* Him! Receiving Him is *knowing* Him! Speaking His Word in love is *knowing* Him! Acting in His love is *knowing* Him!

Acting on what you receive *in Jesus*
is putting what you know into practice!

Begin today! Let's speak out God's Word over ourselves,

our loved ones, our neighbors, our communities … our world!

Speak out in your actions about the extravagant Love of Jesus for all mankind, in the Name of Jesus!

Take back all the devil has ever stolen from you. Use the love of Jesus … the Name of our Lord and Savior in all your talk and walk to stop the enemy! Watch Jesus work on your behalf!

Fill the ears of your heart with His love in Romans 10:17, *"So faith comes by hearing (what is told), and what is heard comes by the preaching (of the message that came from the lips) of Christ (the Messiah Himself)."*

Look up God's Word for yourself!

We hear God's voice …
we have His Faith …
we have the authority of Jesus in us!

Let's USE GOD'S AUTHORITY IN US to take back from the devil! We have the courage of God. He commands us to not be afraid … to be conquerors, *"Have I not commanded you? Be strong, vigorous, and very courageous. Be not afraid, neither be dismayed, for the Lord your God is with you wherever you go!"* Joshua 1:9

Do not be afraid, the Lord your God is always with you *wherever* **you go!**

Have you been robbed? Have you no peace? Have you lost the peace you once had … have you lost your joy, your finances, your health?
Have you yet to find and keep the peace you desperately

want?

A sweet little lady friend of mine says, *"The love of Jesus kicks that sneaky Thief Enemy, the devil, in the 'where it hurts' place!"*

When we know God's Word over every situation in our lives ... when we know the love of Jesus ... when we know Satan is the thief, destroyer and our enemy — not God and not a person of flesh and blood ... *in Jesus,* we *know* we are free!

Let's take a further look at God's Word on this.

God tells us in Ephesians 6:12, *"For WE ARE NOT wrestling with flesh and blood (contending only with physical opponents), BUT against the despotism's (principalities), against the powers, against (the master spirits who are) the world rulers of this present darkness, against the SPIRIT forces of wickedness in the heavenly (supernatural) sphere."*

Satan's demon "buddies" work great in the negative!

Within the spirit world of darkness, Satan rules with his authority! As Satan and his wicked spirit forces (demon cohorts, his "buddies") move about, they strive to get you to wrestle within yourself ... to wrestle with them ... with others ... through the flesh in the natural world realm! Satan works *in* the spirit world as the ruler of darkness!

From within the spiritual realm, through people, through the flesh, in the natural world, wicked spirit forces bait you!

These demon "buddies" make suggestions to you! They

offer you strife and confusion! They try to use you to cause strife and conflicts that will hurt you or hurt others!

Yet, the devil's darkness is no match for you even in your weakest moment because John 1:4, 5 tells us, *"In Him was Life, and the Life was the Light of men. And the Light shines on in the darkness, for the darkness has never overpowered it (put it out or absorbed it or appropriated it, and is unreceptive to it)."*

Rise up with courage. Stop looking at your own abilities, or weakness' and limits ... start looking to God!

You have the Light! You have the "unbeatable power"! You have victories in Jesus!

Satan is the master liar! In his darkest spirit realm he has these master spirits I call demon "buddies", working for him through the natural physical realm in the world.

Yet, try as they may, all the forces of hell can't put out the Light of the world!

The enemy uses his demon spirits (his buddies) to tempt you ... to *try* to deceive you and cause harm to you.

**YOUR ENEMY IS NOT GOD —
NOT YOURSELF — NOT MAN!**

Look again at Ephesians 6:12, *"We do not **wrestle** with **flesh and blood but** against **master spirits, forces of wickedness.**"*

The Bible tells us our enemies

are not flesh and blood!
But are spiritual, master spirits, wicked
and are forces from Satan!

But, *in Jesus*, these master spirits
are *all* defeated!

Romans 8:26 tells us, *"So too the (Holy) Spirit comes to our aid and bears us up in our weakness; for we do not know what prayer to offer nor how to offer it worthily as we ought, but the Spirit Himself goes to meet our supplication and pleads in our behalf .... "*

Listen to the Spirit of God as He helps you! When somebody does you wrong, go after the right enemy!

It happens to all of us! Along the way we've all been hurt, cheated ... lied to ... abused! We can get over it!

It's time you find out you can put the power of God to work for you!

Follow these three simple steps:

1.   **IDENTIFY the enemy.** This is often where we make our biggest blunder. We mistakenly identify our enemy as the person who hurts us! Don't waste your energy or time ranting or raving and plotting to get back at the people who cause you pain. They're simply under the devil's influence. Aim your spiritual ammunition at the right target. Go after the devil; he's behind it all!

2.   **AIM and FIRE!** Once you've got your aim

lined up right, fire! Use the Name and power of Jesus and hit the devil fast and furiously with God's Word! Bind him in the power God has given you! Stop him from doing you any more harm in that area!

3.   **PRAY the prayer of intercession!** This is a final most important part of your steps! Matthew 5:44, 45 tells us, *"Love your enemies, bless them that hate you, and pray for them which despitefully use you, and persecute you; that you may be the children of your Father which is in heaven."*

We have the advantage over the enemy! We are not ignorant of his strife and intentions! We can be forgiving.

2 Corinthians 2:10, 11

Remember, God has great MERCY! Not just for me and you, but for everyone! Acting like the devil and wanting vengeance isn't acting like our Father. I can tell you the devil will think twice before he bothers you again!

Take a stand against strife!
Proverbs 17:14

You see, Satan uses his lying spirits, his demon "buddies", through his negative suggestions in negative thoughts to suggest strife! Just like thoughts and feelings about getting even with someone and not being forgiving. Satan wants you in strife and un-forgiveness!

Then, he begins heckling (provoking) us to start thinking, talking about those suspicious un-forgiving thoughts! As we talk, if we act on those negative feelings and thoughts we're setting ourselves up to get knocked down hard by the enemy.

First, Satan will suggest to you to be fearful or be hurt!

Then he'll suggest to you to criticize and be un-forgiving!

Then he'll heckle you with more negative thoughts on doubting which lead to strife! He'll suggest, and keep suggesting to you to start nursing the negative!

When you nurse the negative ... fear and unbelief follows; then follows anger, hate, sickness, disease, poverty, false pride, selfish ambition, jealousy! All are bombshells set and ready to go off and blow you up!

Don't speak and nurse the negative!

Fear and un-forgiveness lead the way! All these negative strife forces begin with the "heckler". If listened to and nursed along, these negative forces will set up in your heart!

All these negative suggestions and offers come straight out of the lying mouth from the regions of the damned!

Can you see this spiritual realm operating from the flesh with our help through our mouths? With our cooperation, the enemy then can STEAL *and* STEAL again; DESTROY *and* KILL!

"God's words give life ... like a medicine!"

John 6:63
Proverbs 17:22;

The devil is a KILLER! Hold him accountable for the killer that he is! Don't let him bury you "under" circumstances! Use God's life giving Words! His Words are Life!

Proverbs 17:22 tells us, *"A happy heart is good medicine and a cheerful mind works healing ..."*

You bind ... cast down the enemy *with* God's healing Word!

YOU tell the devil, *"NO MORE!"* YOU tell him, *"I belong to God!"*

When you start realizing how overcoming the positive healing Word of God is, coming from your mouth and life, you'll turn off the television, the radio and put down the newspaper.

"Oh Rose," you might be saying, *"that's mighty unreasonable!"*

Yes, it is! But consider this; ***"... you are of God (you belong to Him) and have (already) defeated and overcome them (the agents of the antichrist), because He who lives in you is greater (mightier) than he who is in the world."***

1 John 4:4

Look at it this way ... when someone becomes a doctor he devotes his life to studies and practice as a doctor.

For a excellent doctor, every waking minute is spent reading and studying about, thinking about, talking about ... then practicing and acting on being a doctor!

As a concert pianist, for years I have studied, thought about, and practiced piano for hours every day! Believe me, I have joyfully spent over 50 years fellowshipping with a piano and practicing music!

Child of God let's all study, think about, talk about, act on, and begin to fellowship with all we are in God's Word!

I s it really so unreasonable to practice God's Word? Or, to practice we are God's best that He has created us to be?

Is it so unreasonable to have *intimate* fellowship (friendship) with Jesus … which makes for a *dynamic* relationship with Father God the Creator of all the Universe! Our intimate fellowship makes us *know* Him more excellently … more deeply!

What we fellowship with, we *will* have a relationship with!

One day the Lord spoke to me, *"Rose, everyone talks about having a relationship with Me. I want you to understand, as you have fellowship with Me then you will have a deep relationship with Me!"*

I believe we want to know what our Father's Word is over every circumstance in our lives! We want to know Who Father God is and His Love for us! We all want Jesus and His abundant joy and peace operating in our lives!

But, many times we are fooled! We hook up with fear, despair, or anger! Then we begin to fellowship and hang around with hurt, pain, trouble, and defeat. And the next thing you know we are cryin' and squallin' about how miserable we are!

Do you know that you are who God *says* you are? Do you act and live like who He *says* you are?

You are victorious in Jesus …! Do you talk and walk victoriously? Are you resting in your awesome peace in Jesus?

God's power ... do you *know* you have it?

Honey, when a storm comes into our life ... when the devil raises up to try to kill us, destroy us or our loved ones ... is it then unreasonable to have practiced ... *know* ... and trust we have God's Word? Is it then unreasonable from our mouth and hearts to *depend* on God's Word power?

When storms come we need to have already spent time listening to God day and night, attending to His every Word ... to have been talking with Him!

Honey, it's darn hard to build a house in a hurricane!

Hell trembles as we act on what we read, hear, and believe in God's Word! Hell trembles when we know we *are* in Jesus!

Let's get ahead of the storms! Let's keep the devil discouraged by acting on (practicing) all God teaches us!

We can stop worrying *and we can* be loving *and* forgiving!

Today, I'm confident you can give up worry one minute at a time!

Let's break the worry habit *and* the worry talk with the powerful Word of God!

Let's shake the spiritual realm by walking away from strife and worry! Let's act on God's Words of peace for us!

Today, I'm confident the enemy runs when we talk and walk in the peace of God today!

God says, *"A new heart will I give you and a new spirit will I put within you, and I will take away the stony heart out of your flesh and give you a heart of flesh.*
And I WILL put MY Spirit within you and cause you to walk in MY statutes, and YOU SHALL heed MY ordinances and do them."   Ezekiel 36:26,27

God says, *in Jesus,* He has already given us a new heart and has put *His* Spirit within us and He *causes* us to walk in His love and do His Word! Why would God equip us ... set us free ... and give us His peace and freedom?

So we can lay on the couch and watch hours of television without any pain?

No, no, no! God freed us so we *can* rest and walk in His love! So we *can* receive His forgiveness! So we *can* be forgiving! So we *can go* tell people His Good News and set more captives free ... so we *can* tell them Jesus loves them! God freed us so we *can* love, honor, and glorify Him ... so we *can* love ourselves, and love others!

God has freed us to, *"say continually, Let the Lord be magnified Who takes great pleasure in the prosperity of His servant."*   Psalms 35:27

Father says when we receive His Heart Jesus, He puts
within us *a new* heart —
Child of God, *in JESUS,* we have a *new* heart!

We *have* His Perfect magnified Heart!

God gives us so much in just one scripture promise!

So what can be the problem? Are we ignoring God? Are we ignoring all He has done for us? Are we not "attending" to His Word as He asks in Proverbs 4:20-24? Are we forgiving and loving?

Begin today to *see yourself* **as God sees you;
being loved by Jesus
and being loving and forgiving
to people *and* to yourself!**

Begin today to "attend" to God's Word!

Imagine yourself talking and walking successfully
in the joy of
JESUS AS YOUR STRENGTH!

Visualize yourself STRONG, VICTORIOUS IN HIS LOVE!

Look at things with your *new* heart in God's Spirit in you!

See yourself faithful and at rest with Jesus …
continually walking about,
in peace, talking with Jesus!

Think **of yourself as God says you are;
faithful, prosperous, healed, protected,
successful, delivered,** *and* **made whole!**

As you walk, talking, listening and living *in JESUS* … as your FAITH feeds on His Word … you can receive your HEALING! Whatever your need is … God meets your need by faith! It thrills God to see you walk in faith in Him!

WE HAVE JESUS! We are **re-created**! We *have* His faith His Nature, His Spirit! We are **His re-created** spirits ... *in Him*!

We *have* the very loving, faith nature of God living inside us!

We *are* God's Spirit!

As believers, WE HAVE JESUS LIVING ON THE INSIDE OF US! We are His love! GOD LOVES US and cares for us as His new faith filled ... re-created spirits!

With Jesus, in God's Word, we have all the confidence ever needed in our lives that there is!

- Are you experiencing symptoms of sickness and despair?
- Have doctors diagnosed you with some illness or disease?
- Are you depressed? Angry? Bitter? Un-forgiving?

What does the Word of God say?

"I AM THE LORD WHO HEALS YOU ... who forgives all your iniquities (evil qualities), who heals all your diseases ... !" Praise Him!
Exodus 15:26; Psalms 103:3; 147:3; Isaiah 53; 57:19

Isaiah 53:4-5 speaks loud and clear, *"He has borne our griefs (sicknesses, weaknesses, and distresses) and carried our sorrows and pains (of punishment), yet we (ignorantly) considered Him stricken, smitten, and afflicted by God (as if with leprosy).*

***But He was wounded for our** transgressions, **He was bruised for our** guilt and iniquities**; the** chastisement **(needful to obtain) peace** and **well-being for us** was upon Him, and with the stripes (that wounded) Him we are healed and made whole."*

- Transgressions *(crimes, offences)*
- Guilt *(faults, wrongs)*
- Iniquities *(evil qualities, wickedness)*
- Chastisement *(correction)*

God says in Isaiah 53, Matthew 8, and 1 Peter 2 that 2000 years ago, by the stripes of Jesus we *were* healed *and* made whole! Read these scriptures slowly, over and over, out loud! Ask God to Divinely reveal them to you!

God clearly tells us His Son Jesus *has* borne and *has* healed all our sicknesses and distresses, and He carried all our sorrows and pains off of us. He says we are already healed and made whole!

GOOD NEWS!

In Jesus **you have authority over** *every* **circumstance IN YOUR LIFE!**

Tell me, according to God's Word, how we should be thinking about ourselves, and each other!

According to God's Word tell me how we should think about distress or symptoms or diagnosis of disease and sickness?

"I believe, therefore I speak." 2 Corinthians 4:13

God says, *"Do not fret or have any anxiety about anything, but in every circumstance and in everything, by prayer and petition (definite requests), <u>WITH THANKSGIVING, CONTINUE</u> to make your WANTS known to God ... And God's peace (shall be yours, that tranquil state of a soul assured of its salvation through Christ, and so <u>FEARING NOTHING</u> FROM GOD and being content with its earthly lot of whatever sort that is, that peace) which transcends all understanding shall garrison and mount guard over your hearts and minds in Christ Jesus ... For the rest, brethren, WHATEVER is TRUE, WHATEVER is worthy of reverence and is honorable and seemly, whatever is just, whatever is pure, whatever is lovely and lovable, whatever is kind and winsome and gracious, if there is any virtue and excellence, if there is anything worthy of praise, <u>THINK ON</u> AND WEIGH AND TAKE ACCOUNT OF THESE THINGS (fix your minds on them). <u>Practice</u> what you have learned and received and heard and seen in me, and model your way of living on it ..."*

Faith speaks *and* agrees with God!

Philippians 4:6-9

Child of God, we have got to latch on to the integrity and the credibility of the Word of God over our body, our symptoms, our diagnosis, our minds, our thoughts, our feelings ... our lives! **It is time!** We have got to take our every thought, our every spoken word captive to the Word of God and keep it in check!

When God's Word differs from what our thoughts are or circumstances look like, is that being untruthful? No, not a bit! As we speak, according to God's Word we are speaking faith.

Faith speaking is when I make my words agree with God's Words instead of agreeing with the circumstances around me!

Every evidence of speaking from my mind *and* against my spirit is the lie! A lie occurs when I speak or act in deceit to cause injury.

Charles Capps says the Lord told him this way, *"People can have what they say, but they are saying what they have!"*

Stop telling it like it is!

You *will* get what you say!

This is important. Some people speak God's words but they don't believe and exercise their faith to back up what they say! Then they fall flat on their spiritual faces.

Just wishing or just hoping won't get the job done.

You've got to *"believe!"* You've got to *"receive"* and you've got to *"speak"* in faith believing ... and then *"act"... "believing"!*

Begin today bringing both your tongue and your heart in line with the Word. Start by agreeing with God's Word!

Stop *"telling it like it is"* so to speak and start speaking and believing the promises of God.

Hebrews 11:1 is faith defined, ***"NOW FAITH is the substance of things hoped for, the evidence of things not seen."***

Faith is a substance!
Faith says, *"I have it now!"*

Fear is the perversion of Faith!

Read Proverbs 18:21. Then read
Romans 4:17 ... 2 Corinthians 4:13
"call those things which be not as though they were!"

In the natural physical realm, are you suffering?

Are you diagnosed with sickness or hurting or you're feeling depressed?

Then *attend* to God's Word ... exercise your faith in God's Word ... call forth, speak, profess God's Truth Words of healing over that area.

Praise Him in the mornin'

The truth is ... God's powerful Words of faith are over the natural physical realm. The physical realm has to obey God's spiritual authority!

Praise Him in the evenin'

Call forth, in the Name of Jesus, God's faithful Word over your body and mind! And *keep calling His Word* until you see the manifestation of that Word. REPEAT! Repeat! Repeat God's Word out loud, *"Praise God, I'm healed and made whole. I have the mind and wisdom of Christ! I have no lack! God's Word says so!"*

Praise Him at supper time!

God says, with Prayer (definite request) ... *with* thanksgiving ... *with* Praise's to God ... continue to make your wants known to God! Honey, Faith in Love, created the Universe! Praise in faith *releases* every power God has!

Look again at Philippians 4:6-9! When you speak God's Word over your life … God's peace mounts guard over your heart and mind in Christ Jesus! Walk, stand, sit, sleep, run … live in … His perfect Words in His peace! Can you see the power of God operating through your praise?

Fear nothing *from* God!

Trust everything *to* God!

Begin today
to praise
your Lord and your Savior Jesus!

Read Isaiah 57·19 to confirm God's *power of praise*!

Remember Philippians 4:6-9 says, *"Do not fret or have any anxiety about anything, but in every circumstance and in everything, by prayer and petition (definite requests), with thanksgiving, continue to make your wants known to God."*

"THINK (FIX your mind) **with thanksgiving** *… ON THESE THINGS, things that are … "*

- *TRUE*
- *WORTHY OF REVERENCE*
- *HONORABLE*
- *SEEMLY*
- *JUST*
- *PURE*
- *LOVELY*

- *LOVABLE*
- *KIND and WINSOME*
- *GRACIOUS*
- *ANY VIRTUE*
- *EXCELLENCE*
- <u>*ANYTHING WORTHY OF PRAISE*</u>

Honey, Jesus is *all* of the above! He is Praise … think on Jesus!
Philippians 4:6-9

Say out loud, *"I praise you Lord … I can THINK ON and weigh and take account of these things!"*

FIX … PRACTICE … PRAISE
(to place so that part is tightly surrounded,
embed, root, sink)

FIX **YOUR MIND** *ON* **JESUS**
and OFF **your circumstances!** *Practice* **praise!**

No matter what your circumstances look like … you think about, speak out loud, talk about, practice, and praise God *in faith, **in all things**,* believing … all day … on that particular scripture in His Word that covers your circumstance!

Begin now to Praise the Lord! Speak these praises out loud!

"I PRAISE you God for ALL Your Love for me … for Jesus! Jesus is ALL for me! Jesus is Faithful!" John 3:35, 36; 13:35; Ephesians 3:19; 2 Corinthians 5:14, 15; Philippians 1:10, 11

"I PRAISE You Jesus! Thank You Jesus for Who You are and for all You have already done for me!"
Ephesians 12:20; Philippians 4:19

"I PRAISE You Jesus that You have forgiven, redeemed, and blessed me eternally from every sin I have committed and could ever commit!"   Mark 3:27; Romans 4:7; 1 John 2:12

"I PRAISE You God for Your total provision and protection for me from all harm according to Psalms 91!" (Read *out loud* and stand praising, believing Father God for Psalms 91 and 103).

"I PRAISE You God for every perfect breath I breath, not just for the day or the week I walk in!"   Psalms 150:6

"I PRAISE You Lord Jesus for my Divine health, and Divine mind that You have given me!"   Isaiah 53

"I PRAISE You Father that You repeatedly spoke in five books of the Bible about how You and Jesus are alive inside me, and I am One with You!"

"I PRAISE You Father, as a believer, I can walk, talk, listen to, and always have You with me; 1,000%, un-limited ... all the time!"   John 15:5, 7, 10

Keep your union
with Jesus intact!

Every thing else
will be taken care of!

PRAISE Father and Jesus of the Universe ... that you *are* the Son or Daughter of the Most High Living God, Lord and Savior ... The Creator!   Genesis—Revelation

PRAISE Him that you are His very own child! Praise God He is your Father!   Matthew 7:11

PRAISE JESUS He is your Savior, Lord, Good Shepherd *and* Deliverer! Praise Him you are His Bright Light!
Matthew 9:22; Luke 13:16; John 12:15; 2 Corinthians 6:18

PRAISE YOUR FATHER GOD that ... *in JESUS* ... the enemy Satan was and *is* eternally paralyzed, broken, and defeated!   Colossians 2:15; Hebrews 2:14

PRAISE the Lord Jesus, that *in Him*, you are set free from all bondages! Praise Him that you have total authority and victory over the enemy, and every circumstance in your life!
Luke 9:1; 10:19; 19:17; 2 Corinthians 10:8; 1 Timothy 2:2-6

"I PRAISE You Lord that I am set free and can live in Your righteous ABUNDANT PROSPEROUS LIFE that You promised me!"

Wake up to your righteousness in Christ Jesus!

In the Name of Jesus, you are in right standing with God. You have authority over *every* circumstance in your life! Begin, praising and giving in abundance! God *will* rebuke the devourer for your sake! Praise and worship Him for it!   Malachi 3:11, 12

And should anyone want to complain, or criticize you for your over-whelming praise or love of your Jesus, silence them by your well doing!   1 Peter 2:15

Read all of Colossians 2:9-15 as you awake to your righteousness (right standing) in Jesus! Verse 20 tells us we have died *with Christ and we no longer belong to this world!*

Remember, Father God, *and* Jesus are always faithful!

They have ALL Faith *in* you!

JESUS IS YOUR PRAISE!

SATAN IS THE HECKLER!

Satan is the *defeated* tempter!

This fantastic list of scriptures are for your encouragement and edification! These scriptures will begin to further build your faith, knowledge, and understanding of Who God is and of God's faith *in you* and *for you* …
I ask for God's Divine revelation of His Word for you!

Read out loud slowly every day these rich powerful scriptures … let God, through His Word, build your spirit and mind into His mountain moving faith … read, read, read … do, do, and do some more …

Psalms 91
Psalms 103:1-5
Isaiah 53:3-5
Isaiah 54:8-17
Mark 5:36
Luke 2:49
John 1:1, 3
Acts 14:3; 15:11
Romans 3:21, 26; 4:16; 5:1-2, 21; 10:8-10
1 Corinthians 1:3
2 Corinthians 3:4-5; 5:17; 9:9-11; 12:9, 10
Galatians 2:16, 20; 3:14, 22, 26

Ephesians 1:1-23; 2:7, 8, 9; 3:8-**12, 14-21**; 4:4, 5-8;
        6:16, **23**

Colossians 1:0-14; 2:5-7
1 Timothy **1:14, 15**; 3:13
2 Timothy 1:13
Hebrews 4:3; **12:1-2**
James 1:5-6; 2:1
2 Peter 1:1-4; 3:18

Jude 1:20

"And the grace (unmerited favor and blessing) of our Lord (actually) flowed out superabundantly and beyond measure for me, accompanied by faith and love that are (to be realized) in Christ Jesus."

CHAPTER 5

GOD & JESUS
ARE FAITHFUL!
~
SATAN *IS*
THE DEFEATED TEMPTER!
Matthew 4:3, 4

Honey, Jesus was hungry! Jesus had just spent 40 days and nights in the wilderness (desert) without food, where He was tried *exceedingly* by the devil! ***"Then the devil said to Him, 'IF you are God's Son, command these stones to be made (loaves of) bread'.***

And Jesus said, 'IT IS written, Man shall not live and be upheld and sustained by (on) bread alone, but by every word that comes forth from the mouth of God'." Luke 4:2-4

40 days and 40 nights with no food ... JESUS WAS HUNGRY! He was hungry for physical food! BUT, He was filled to over-flowing with confidence in His Father's Word!

Jesus knew the devil is the defeated tempter! Still, the enemy always aims at what he thinks is our deepest weakness!

Realize, at that desert edge, with the agony of hunger ravaging His body, Jesus made a choice! Jesus made a Godly decision!

Jesus decided to submit, to stand on, and to speak out Father God's Word! He decided to resist the devils temptation!

He decided to boldly, speak out Father God's written Word from His mouth, and Spirit.

The devil had already *exceedingly* tried and tested Jesus for 40 days *and* 40 nights. Now he was challenging Jesus to actually turn rocks into bread, and eat!

The physical hunger needs of Jesus were tremendous! Jesus made a choice; He made a decision!

Have you ever faced such a temptation as this? Have there been circumstances in your life that seemed unbearable ... no longer tolerable? Has the devil ever tempted you to turn a hard rock circumstance into a warm bread feast, and turn your back on God's Word, and not trust His provisions?

Any Child of God who is breathing has had the opportunity offered to them to look at their circumstances and ask themselves, *"Am I going to believe my Father and His Word to provide for me; OR, am I going to listen to my feelings and my thoughts ... am I going to look at my circumstances, and look at and go by what I can physically feel and see?"*

The decision had to be made! The only successful, great decision and choice for Jesus to make was that He speak God's Word ... then stand on it over those agonizing circumstances.

Decide *to* decide!

Can you imagine what the outcome would have been if Jesus had decided to listen to the devil ... look only at His circumstances ... or act only on His feelings? Or, what would have happened if Jesus had said or done nothing?

As we trust God and speak the Word of God, His Word becomes a literal feast to our mind and spirit, like bread food is to our body!

We can trust Father God as we speak His Words of Life instead of Death, over our every circumstance, we can stand in faith on God's Word.

Jesus decided to feast on His Fathers Word!

Jesus *knew* He could trust His Father!

Jesus expected His Father to meet His every need! He expected God to correctly *and* abundantly feed Him ... physically, mentally, spiritually!

Jesus, as physically hungry as He was, straightout told the devil, *"Man does not live by bread alone but will "live" by every Word from God's mouth!"* Jesus quoted Deuteronomy 8:3 to the devil!

You might say, *"Well Rose, Jesus was the Son of God. He was able to resist these temptations of the enemy because He's powerful ... He's Jesus!"*

Your right! This is true! Jesus is The powerful Son of God.

And, Child of God, through the same power Jesus has ...

... you *are* the powerful Son or Daughter of God!
2 Corinthians 6:17

2 Peter 2:9 strongly tells us, *"... the Lord knows how to rescue the godly out of temptations and trials ...!"*

God is OUR Father! As His children, *with* *Jesus***, we have His same authority and abilities!** Decide to not allow Satan to sneak up on you! Don't let the devil talk louder than your faith words can talk!

Words are serious business!

Decide to not let the devil keep you ignorant of Father's power and Word for you! Decide to speak the Word of God loud and clear in the face of your circumstances!

Start agreeing with God's Word! **Don't agree with the devil! Don't let him rip you off of Father's Word already living inside you!**

SPEAK, PRAY THE WORD out loud over your situation!

"And this is the confidence (the assurance, the privilege of boldness) which we have in Him: (we are sure) that if we ask anything (make any request) according to His will (in agreement with His own plan), He listens to and hears us!"
1 John 5:14

Therefore, what you say in prayer is the key to getting your prayers answered. You must communicate to God in faith believing what He has already communicated in His Word to you ... fully assured that your prayers will have results.

Apply faith pressure!

Our love and faith, our receiving and giving, is *from* God! *FROM* GOD! Just like it is from God to Jesus! Is God's power or Word for us any less than it is to Jesus? Absolutely not!

Hebrews 10:23 tells us we are to *"hold fast to our profession, our confession of faith without wavering; (for He is faithful that promised)."*

God is faithful! *Through Jesus*, in God's Word, God sees to it that His Words and seeds of strength are sown into our new good ground of our re-born, re-created hearts!

Confess God's Word and watch Him work!

It is our privilege to glorify God! With God we make the things we desire come to pass. So don't speak words of doubt and unbelief! Don't ask with wrong purpose or evil selfish motives (James 4:3). CONFESS … profess … THE WORD! When we diligently seek the Lord and continue confessing and seeding words of faith over our life, God will reward our efforts.   Hebrews 11:6

Satan will always attempt to rob us; to steal from us … to steal God's Word, our seeds!

He'll try to get us to use words of fear or chit-chat or defeat in circumstances in order to kill and steal God's Word!

You have Keys … God's Word power to use to bind & *loose!*
Matthew 16:19

The defeated enemy tries to steal right out from under our noses! He'll try us just like he tried to steal from Jesus at that desert edge! But, we have the Keys to the Kingdom … Keys to use … let's use them!

We have God's Word Power Keys! Don't you ever accept doubt and fear again!

Use your Word Keys to flip God's faith power switch on! Then, watch Him turn on His power over your life and see the devil run!

L et's give all praise to Jesus, our promised Love ... our Savior and Lord ... our Protector and Provider!

Look at your words!
Are your words fearful or faithful?

Praise Father God, that in the power of Jesus, by His Faith you won't listen to the devil and he's not allowed to rob you any further!

The enemy won't *and* can't steal, kill, and destroy from our lives ... *if we don't let him*!

Pray, talk to God! Use these seven scripture guides to exercise God's fearless Word power! PRAYER WORKS ...

You can make prayer work:

1. **Speak the Word ... the answer ... *not* the problem!**
   Isaiah 55:11

   2. **Apply faith pressure!**   Hebrews 10:23

   3. **Don't ever accept doubt or fear!**
   Ephesians 6:11; 2 Corinthians 10:5
   4. **Visualize success *and* reject failure.**
   Psalms 107:2
   5. **Testify what you believe!**   John 14:13, 14

   6. **Be a blessing!**   Galatians 6:2

   7. **Love ... give, *and* you will receive!**
   Luke 6:38; James 5:16

Satan tries! But only with our submission *to* him *in* our agreement *with* him is he ever able to get us into speaking words in an attitude of fear, despair or defeat!

I am convinced according to James 3:2-7 that by the words of our mouth, lined up with the powerful Word of God, we can set worlds on fire with curses ... or we extinguish every flame! We can set people free, from all bondages who are held captive ... to love, live, give, and have life abundantly in Jesus in His Name!

Start out taking baby steps. Then move on into walking ... then running. God will build you up to your running strength and confidence!

Remember, when you speak words of fear or you listen to or act (walk) with the devil ... you are listening to ... you are walking with the Killer, the Destroyer!

Just like Jesus did, without any fear ... begin speaking and giving God's Word!

SPEAK God's Word ... in love over your circumstances!

Examine God's Word! Examine your words! Words are actions! Examine your actions! **At all costs, be a blessing!**

Do your words and actions match up to God's Words?

Jesus tells us, *"I will give you the keys of the kingdom of heaven; and whatever you bind (declare to be improper and unlawful) on earth must be what is already bound in heaven; and whatever you loose (declare lawful) on earth must be what is already loosed in heaven."*   Matthew 16:19

You have the very *Keys* of the kingdom … you have the power word *Keys* of Jesus to use … to bind *and* loose with your mouth … everything that is already bound and loosed in heaven!

You hold the very *Keys* of Death (fear *and* hate) *and* Life (love) in your mouth!

You have the ability (power), *in Jesus,* to bind poverty, sickness, disease, despair … every evil, negative force on this earth! Because these things are absolutely already bound in heaven.

You have the ability (power), *in Jesus* to loose every good thing of God … faith, prosperity, divine health, a sound mind, wisdom, love, every godly, positive force on this earth! Because these things are absolutely already loose in heaven!

God's Words are Life *and* health coming from your mouth!

Jesus, while praying to His Father, said to Peter in Luke 22:31-32, *"… LISTEN! Satan has asked excessively that (all of) you be given up to him (out of the power and keeping of God), that he might sift (all of) you like grain, <u>but I have prayed</u> especially for you (Peter), that your (own) faith may not fail; and when you yourself have turned again, strengthen and establish your brethren."*

Read this scripture again … slowly … out loud! Do you see Jesus using God's powerful words to resist the excessive, persistence of the enemy? Do you see the importance for you to *read* and *study* and *know* and *speak* God's Word for yourself?

Read what Jesus tells us again, *"Listen! Satan has asked excessively that ALL of you be given up to him (out of the power and keeping of God) ... he wants to sift all of you like grain ... !"*

ALL of us, Child of God, ALL! Satan asked *excessively* to sift us ALL!

The devil asked excessively to *sift* us, measure us out ... mark us off!

Sift us like grain means to measure, to weigh it out, to mark it off! Satan wants to mark us all off!

But, Jesus prayed the power of God to keep ALL of us! The enemy can not have us, *unless we let him,* because Jesus prayed! Jesus prayed our faith not fail and Jesus prayed for God to keep us ... the enemy can not sift us or have us unless we agree!

God *IS* a faith 'builder' *NOT* a faith 'sifter'!

Earlier, before this, Jesus had told Peter that he would deny Him 3 times. Jesus knew Peter! Jesus knew all about what Peter would do before he did it! Jesus always knows what all of us will do before we do it! God gave us all knowing Jesus! Jesus also knows He has given us His heart! We have His heart! Jesus knows all about our circumstances!

I remember the first time I understood Jesus knows *everything* about me. It's a humbling, and exciting experience.

Yes, Jesus knows what we'll do before we do. He wants us to *know* Him! He wants us to *know* ourselves *in Him*!

Jesus wants us to know ourselves! He wants us to know what we can do *through Him*; what we can and will do *in Him*! Jesus wants us to know what He has already done for us ... !

Give the devil *no* permit to kill!

Jesus wants us to *know* that we *know* we can walk in faith without fear! Jesus wants us to *know* that we *know* we can trust Him to safely guide us! He safely leads us!

In the opposite, the devil wants to confuse us and kill us! He is THE Confuser and THE Killer!

And Jesus said, *"... but I HAVE PRAYED especially for you Peter that your (own) FAITH may NOT FAIL; and when YOU yourself HAVE TURNED again, STRENGTHEN AND ESTABLISH your BRETHREN."*   Luke 22:32

Read and LISTEN closely! Jesus prayed! Jesus talks to God about us! God listens! Remember, God already knows us as His beloved and what we will do! Jesus loved Peter and He knew Peter loved Him!

Jesus *knows* everything *about* every thing *and* every body!

Jesus prayed to Father God about Peter *and* us. When Jesus prayed, He already knew what Peter would do!

Jesus was seeding ... He was seeding and confirming His Word into Peter's heart!

Not only did Jesus pray for Peter; Jesus prays for us! Earlier, Jesus told Peter that out of fear, Peter would deny even knowing Him 3 times in one night! But, Jesus knew Peter's faith and heart. Jesus already *knew* Peter loved Him, and that he would turn again to Him.

Jesus already had faith in Peter. Jesus knew that He could trust Peter! He knew that Peter would turn! Jesus knew that He would build His Church on Peter's faith, and love for Him!

Matthew 16:18

Jesus was telling Peter, *"I know what you will do."*

Jesus was telling Peter, *"I know your faith Peter, and your weaknesses ... I love you."*

Go back and slowly read again, out loud, Luke 22:32! Let the Holy Spirit reveal the depth of this scripture to you!

Jesus *knows* us!
He has faith *in us* ... He loves us!

Jesus *knows* we are faithful ...
in Father's Eyes we are perfect !

You see, Jesus loved Peter! Jesus wanted Peter to see himself as God sees him! Jesus already knew that Peter deeply loved Him from his heart!

God hears Jesus pray!

Peter, or his faith,
did not fail Jesus!

Peter, out of fear, allowed *his* faith to *weaken!* **PETER, or his faith, COULD NOT FAIL!** *In Christ* we do not fail!

In Christ there can be no failure!

Failure means to fold up, go under, close down, flop!

Peter did not fold up, go under, close down or flop … and neither do we!

In Luke 22: 56-62, we learn that Peter, in his fear, denied even knowing Jesus … not once, not twice, but three times!

Then, *"And the Lord turned and looked at Peter. And Peter recalled the Lord's words, how He had told him, before the cock crows today, you will deny Me thrice. And Peter went out, and wept bitterly (that is, with painfully moving grief)."*

Oh yes, Peter wept! He was so close to Jesus that he could look into the loving, forgiving Eyes of his all knowing, giving Christ.

In Christ **there can be no failure!**

When Peter looked into those Beautiful forgiving, loving eyes of Jesus, when Peter saw The Truth … when he remembered what Jesus had said … when he remembered Jesus' Words of trust over him … when Peter remembered how deeply Jesus loved him … when Peter remembered how Jesus knew his heart and he remembered how forgiving Jesus is …

Peter wept bitterly
(with painfully moving grief)!

Peter's faith may have weakened, but Peter, or his faith, or the faith of Jesus in Peter, could never fail.

Jesus had already prayed that Peter's faith would not fail!

Yes! Peter looked into the Beautiful, loving, forgiving, faithful Eyes of Jesus! He remembered how Jesus loved him ... had prayed for him ... then he wept bitterly!

When Peter wept, he turned! Peter turned, and later he went forth to minister the love, salvation, and healing of Christ to thousands. Peter ministered, strengthened and established the brethren, just like Jesus said he would!   Acts 5:15, 16; 9:34, 40, 41; 10:33

> **When it comes time to turn — then we'll turn baby, we'll turn!**

The New Testament is full of God's Great Hand on Peter's worldwide evangelistic ministry work! There were 3,000 in his first meeting!

Look back at that blessed, but horrible hour closing in on Jesus at His crucifixion time ... Jesus turned to look at Peter!

Remember, Jesus was yet to be crucified, die, and be resurrected!

Peter would experience first-hand God's great full plan! He would see what salvation, redemption, and what his life *in Christ* would mean.

God built His church on the faith and love of Jesus in Peter ... this was the faith and love that Jesus knew Father God had for Peter. He placed that love in Peter's heart!

We can see Peter's loving heart first-hand! Baby, is it time to turn? Is it time to turn around to look into the eyes of Jesus?

Have we ignored God's love and plans for us? Have we listened to the devil's suggestions, his lies, to make us fearful? Let's be frank … we all have!

Let's remember and understand … Satan, *not God*, is in the "faith sifting" … "faith tearing down" … "faith destroying" … "mark you off"… "faith killing" business! It's the devil's job, his work! But, Honey, never you mind the defeated devil!

God, our Father, has plans for us!
He believes in us!

Our God is in the 'faith building' …
'faith protecting' …
'faith keeping' …
'believing' … 'providing' business!

Have you ever noticed yourself while under attack from the enemy as he *tries* to tempt you, measure you out, and sift you like wheat? Let's be honest! We all have listened to the devil! It's not a pretty sight!

Through ignorance, or willful disobedience, we have all denied God's Word, and our loving Christ!

We have denied the Saving Power living inside of us! We have denied the Healing power of Jesus living inside us! We have ignored His abundant freedom, provisions and His protection over us!

The devil says, *"whoo-pee"*, every time you listen to him!

We have all denied God's Word ... we have ignored Jesus!

T he enemy has attempted to distract us all from God's love! We have all denied, or ignored, the powerful Love of Jesus for us at one time or another!

We have all listened to, and followed the lies of the devil and waltzed right into acting on his suggestions to be fearful, doubtful, hurt, hurtful, hateful, deceitful, stressed out, worried, depressed, condemned, sick, angry, confused ... *un-forgiving!*

We have all listened to the *"whoo-pee talk"* as I call it!

We have all denied the awesome, forgiving love of our Christ!

As some people say, *"Let's be honest"!*

Well beloved, we have all been weak and walked in ignorance of God's word; we all have!

Honey, if you depend on your feelings, or emotions ... instead of Jesus ... you'll be a wreck !

A nd, just like Peter, when I finally *looked* into the *loving, forgiving, faithful, Beautiful Eyes of Jesus* ... I have painfully wept ... and I turned!

In ignorance, and by choice we have all listened to Satan at one time or another! And, we can all stop listening to the lies of the devil!

I use to talk about, and very sincerely write about, *my feelings*! I was crying out, struggling to be brave in my human emotions!

I wrote about and I wallowed in every hurt, confused, and angry *feeling* of human emotion I had. I was making every mental, natural flesh, sense knowledge effort I knew how to just get through every pain I felt; pains I was allowing myself to live in.

I was not listening to God's healing love for me! I did not weigh out my thoughts or my feelings next to God's Word!

I had faithful God's Spirit! I had His extravagant Love Jesus, and His powerful Word, buried under years and mountains of feelings of fear, and hopelessness.

Years ago, for several painful years, during a divorce, I cried out about *my feelings* in Christian counseling every week!

I spent hours thinking and talking about *my feelings*. I was working diligently to get through *my feelings, my hurts,* and that devastating divorce!

I would cry out to God, but I wasn't listening to God's Word! I was trying to get rid of great pain. And let's be reminded here, sometimes as all the birds (parties) work together ... all the birds can be flying in the wrong direction!

We are not to follow, or try to control, the desires or wills of other people!

If where you are or what you feel is in conflict with God's Word ... STOP ... line *yourself* up with God's Word!

In the past, as I ignored God's Word, ignored His Love, ignored His total Provision and His Forgiveness, ignored His Grace and Mercy ... I was living and keeping my eyes constantly on *my* fears ... *my* hurt feelings!

Are you sick *and* tired of wakin' up sick *and* tired?

Some time following this divorce, in deep despair, in the throws of health and financial disasters ... I clearly, audibly heard my Lord Jesus say, *"Rose, how much more are you going to let the devil have?"*

I felt like I was at the bottom of the barrel. My blessed Mother actually said to me, *"Honey, you are not at the bottom of the barrel, you are under the barrel."*

The words to an old Willie Nelson song, *"I'm Sick and Tired of Wakin' up Sick and Tired"* began to ring a loud bell! I took one very short, last look at my angry, hurt, un-forgiving feelings.

When what your feeling or living in is contrary to God's love or Word for you ... get out ... and get out fast!

Later, when I learned worry, strife, fear, and a whole lot else I was doing was contrary to the Word of God ... one day I said, *"ENOUGH IS ENOUGH!"*

Finally, I was done! I was done with hurt feelings ... done with wrong thinking ... done with living in my feelings, and listening to wrong defeated talk! I was done wakin' up sick and tired!

One day, by God's grace, I *chose* to get out from under the barrel … I *chose* to stop living in fearful, hurt feelings and feeling pitiful, afraid, and feeling left in a rubble of defeat.

Finally, by God's merciful grace, I *chose* Life … His Life! With God's love, I *chose* to walk and live in God's Word … I *chose* to live in His joy, and peace, and love of Jesus.

By the mercy of God, I *chose* to latch on to the grace and peace of God! Peace I had heard about but knew I wasn't living in! By God's grace and prayers of devoted faithful loved ones, I *chose* to begin loving the un-loveable! I wanted to be forgiving … move on … forget the past! I had to *choose* to receive God's forgiveness, and love for me! I *chose* to be forgiving! In the joy of the Lord, I began receiving and giving Jesus and His forgiveness, and His love away!

"Thank you Jesus for loving us even when we think we aren't lovable, and can't love You or anybody!"

You *are* the man or woman God *knows* you to be!

One day, by the mercy of God, I stopped being fed up and led around by feeling fearful, doubtful, hurt, angry … riding on a high horse of depressed and defeated *feelings*!

I chose to listen to the mercy and grace of my Father! I looked away from *me and my feelings* into the merciful, forgiving, loving, faithful Beautiful Eyes of Jesus and His love!

Thank God, *with Jesus,* one day, by the grace of God, I knew I could look past *my* hurt feelings, *my* fears, *my* angers, *and my* success'!

Philippians 3:13, 14, ***"... but one thing I do, forgetting what lies behind and straining forward to what lies ahead, I press on toward the goal to win the (supreme and heavenly) prize to which God in Christ is calling us upward!"***

By God's mercy, He showed me *my* despair, *my* past, *my* depressions, *my* doubts, *my* confusion, *my* past, *my* sorrows ... *all* losses ... *and* success' were just that ... *mine!* Jesus showed me that *in Him* they are gone ... in the past! He says, ***"PRESS ON!"***

Yes, we can *press on ... press on ... press on*! Jesus shows us that we are who He says we are. We are not whatever memories we may have of ourselves ... or others, negative or positive!

I *refuse* to listen to Satan's tricks and lies any longer!

Arc you willing ... by God's grace, to press on, look to Jesus, past your past, beyond *your*-self?

Let's praise Father God, because of Jesus, we can stop looking at circumstances and start looking into the never changing, faithful, Beautiful Eyes of Jesus in God's Word! With Jesus, we *can* press on ... into victory with Him!

Standing in Jesus, and pressing on in His loving, powerful Word is a guaranteed victory!

The day we begin to *receive* His Word and abundant provisions is the day we believe *and* we receive the love *our* Jesus has for us ... and for all mankind!

We can receive that Jesus is Who He says that He is ... and that we are who God knows us to be! We are who He says that we are!

We can receive that Jesus knows us, and He loves us! We can receive that Jesus knows that we love Him … God tells us this in 1 John 4:19, *"Because I first loved you, you love Me!"* Yes, because Father God first loved us … we love Him.

How often does the enemy try to steal this Word from us?

Father *planned* His Victorious abundant, prosperous Life of extravagant love in Jesus for us! YES! Father GREATLY *planned* His ALL for us! Have we accepted *His great plans* for us?

Have you only heard about Jesus? Do you want to *know*, and *see the heart of* Jesus?

Are you crying out to stop fearing … feeling hurt, worried, depressed … sick? Are you weeping to *know* that you *know* Jesus?

We all weep in His Love when we realize that we have been listening and acting on our feelings in the enemies suggestions to worry, and deny the love of our Christ!

Are you ready to *know* that you can *know* Jesus?

Because of the extravagant love and grace, and mercy of Jesus … we can *know* His abundant life He plans for us! We can *live in* Jesus Christ!

You can decide today to get to *know* … *better than ever* … Jesus Christ greater than ever before! Ask Him to help you! Jesus is your giving, loving Lord! He's your *Good* Shepherd!

As a believer, Precious Child of God, Good Jesus is alive! He lives inside you! (John 14; 17; 20).

Begin today to *diligently* read God's Word! Ask Jesus to reveal Himself to you! Ask God to reveal His Word to you!

Jesus will guide you in all His wisdom safely! You can walk victoriously in His Love! He is your Great Deliverer ... your freedom you are looking for!

We don't have to live life struggling! We don't have to live life like we're defeated Christians!

I am confident God Loves ME! I am confident He loves YOU!

I have seen God! He says we have seen Him!

John 14:23; 17:23; 1 John 4:15-17

I am confident God loves you! I am confident that God is all good! I am confident that God's Word is the Truth!

Seek and hold fast to Jesus! Hold fast to God's Kingdom, and His Righteousness living inside you. You have the very Mind of Christ! You have His Wisdom! Let's start today to stand on God's Word and begin to speak from His Mind!

God's Wisdom
is
His righteousness
in operation!

Psalms 107:2 says, *"Let the redeemed of the Lord say so, whom He has delivered from the hand of the enemy!"*

We are delivered from the hand of the enemy. We are the redeemed, righteous believers, *and* receivers of our loving Jesus! Let's *say so!*

As believers, WE ARE *IN* CHRIST! Let's *say so!*

As believers, we are *God's righteousness IN CHRIST*! Let's *say so!*

CHRIST IS LIVING and ALIVE *INSIDE YOU*! *Say so!*

You are the redeemed of the Lord! Whatever you say is so!

You are the Beloved Daughter or Son of our Father God!
LET'S SAY SO!

Through Jesus, in His Grace … in His Word of His Love for us, God has made His love abundantly clear to us! *Let's say so!*

Beloved, through His Grace … in His wisdom in the power of the Holy Spirit … we can listen, believe and receive all He has for us!

Now let's confess, *say so … act* on His Lordship over us!

In Jesus, what a victorious life of love *with Jesus* we now have!

What a victorious life of love *with Jesus* we can take hold of, and live in! Choose today to live in your Victory Life *with Jesus*!

God's Word says, *"While we were yet sinners God commanded His Love toward us."*

"I am now in Christ! We are in Christ, He is in us!" Let's say so!   Romans 5:8

Just like Peter, John, Matthew, Mark, Paul and so many others, we are *in Christ* … He is *in* us … *in Jesus* we are God's righteous, blessed, loved, and strengthened! Let's *say so!*

In Jesus, in God's Word, we are completely *set free* from fear, anxiety, tragedy, disease, sickness, poverty, lack, depression, anger, bitterness, hopelessness! Let's say so, and talk about it from Isaiah 53:3-5, Matthew 8:17, and 1 Peter 2:24!

In Jesus, just like Peter, we can strengthen and establish our Brothers and Sisters in God's Love and Word! *In Jesus*, we can speak God's Word and set them free from the enemy! Let's *say so!*

In Jesus, **we are set free from every attempt of the enemy being successful ...**

LET'S SAY SO!
LET'S TALK ABOUT JESUS!

There are over 140 scriptures on who we are and what we are and what we have *in Christ* in the New Testament! Just begin going through your Bible underlining scriptures that read, *in Him, in Whom, through Him, by Him, of Him, in Jesus, and you will be amazed..*

"You know, God sends tragedy to make us stronger!"

"What kind of God does that?"

Without the correct knowledge *of* God's love for you or His Word ... you will believe and act on things you hear (or have heard) through tradition or religious circles. There are old time traditions ... religious ideas that steal the power of the promises of God.

In the past I have actually said, and I have heard other people say things like, *"God may send tragedy to teach you ... to make you stronger."* Or, *"It's not always God's will to heal you!"*

"God never did promise to deliver us out of troubles."

"He may send troubles to make us more like Jesus."

"Healing has passed away. God can get glory from Christians being sick!"

These traditional statements may sound right, but it is not right. It is not what God's Word says. In fact, according to God's Word, these statements are absolutely opposite to what God's Word says! They sound utterly foolish.

Jesus tells us in Matthew 15:6, ***"So for the sake of your tradition (the rules handed down by your forefathers), you have set aside the Word of God (depriving it of force and authority and making it of no effect)."***

Many people set God's Word aside and stand on their own beliefs!

Jesus has already conquered the world! Jesus said so in John 16:33, ***"I have told you these things, so that in Me you may have (perfect) peace and confidence. In the world you have tribulation and trials and distress and frustration: but be of good cheer (take courage; be confident, certain, undaunted!) For I have overcome the world. (I have deprived it of power to harm you and have conquered it for you.)***
John 14:27; 17:17

Tragedy, despair, death ... disease ... are not used ... or needed by God ... as great, positive teachers —

If tragedy was such a great teacher, all the world should be rejoicing! We could totally, completely trust in tragedy ... and all the suffering world could and would be in love with Divine God's so called concept of tragedy.

Honey, if sickness, disease, and despair were God's Will then the world should be delighted to be in His Will, suffering, dying of disease, and destruction! This is old time traditional thinking and superstitions.

I have yet to meet one sick, diseased, despaired, destroyed, physically, emotionally hurting or mentally ill person in my life that was truly thankful to be in a tragic suffering condition! Most suffering people are desperately wanting, seeking, *hoping, or trying to do everything possible* to be healed, set free, or at least better!

Let's break down these old traditions with God's Truth in God's Word!

Let's deliver a hurting world from the most dangerous killer of all … the killer of tradition!

I can tell you for a fact, I don't want any more suffering in my life … nor will I ever again receive the right for any more tragedy, pain, sickness, diseases, mental or physical, financial suffering, emotional suffering, or loss or despair to dwell in my body, or over my life.

Sickness and disease are a tragedy!

The Jesus that saved me is the Jesus that … protects me, richly provides for me … and is my Most High Refuge.   Psalms 91; 103

We can *trust* God's Good Life! We don't need to *fear* God's Good Life!   Psalms 91; Philippians 4:19

Fear of God's *Good Life* is a greater tragedy!

By God's direction and grace, I *attend* to God's Word, meditate day and night on God's Word, and walk in His faith and love … !

By God's Grace I intend to live in the prosperous, abundant provided, protected peaceful, loving arms of my Father, just like He plans for all of us! Read these powerful, freeing Words of God in Proverbs 4:23; Joshua 1:8.

Mercy House / Rose Leibundguth Ministries, churches, hospitals, doctor offices, mental health facilities, crisis centers, emergency clinics ... all are full of suffering people crying out for hope and relief! People all over the world are hoping, crying out, and searching for every possible avenue or answer in research laboratories, seeking spirituality, and intellectual knowledge to relieve them of human despair, and suffering!

Everyone is seeking answers on *how* to get well, stay well, get help, and to be free of pain and misery.

JESUS IS THE ANSWER!

If people really think God needs to or wants to use despair, sickness or death to teach us some great godly truth, then why are people trying to get better?

Let's all just stay sick, and depressed so God can teach us, and we can learn! Let's let what *we think* is God's will be done! And you know what, some people do just that!

And yes, we may learn during tragedy! Yes, we cry out to God in times of despair and tragedy! And yes, God comforts us.

But, tragedy is not a tool God needs to use to teach us His love!

In God's plans, His Will for us, His love, provision and peace for us ... lives protecting, delivering Jesus! Jeremiah 29:11

Sickness and tragedy are like sour lemons! They can even become a best friend! In fact, that is all some people can talk about … how sour *their* lemon is!

Deep down, we *know* in God's Word and in our spirit that it is not God's Divine will for us to be sick, fearful, worried or to suffer! God's Word says so in John 14:27; 16:33, and Malachi 3:6!

Jesus *overcame* the world for us! Remember Exodus 15:26 and Malachi 3:6; *"God never changes!"* God does not want us to suffer.

When Jesus talks about suffering … the suffering that Christ was talking about was His suffering … the rejection of Him. His suffering was, and is, when people refuse Him!

Read out loud Psalms 25 and clear up for yourself this whole wrong idea of suffering once and for all!

Learn to live in Jesus, God's circle of blessing and prosperity especially in God's Word in verses 10, 12 and 13, 14, 20, 21!

How foolish it is for people to think God keeps bringing despair on us only to keep bringing us out of despair!

God's Divine will, according to His Word, offers every one of us His Divine prosperity in health, mind, and spirit … !

It is written many times in God's Word! He speaks clearly about giving us His *Good Life! He gave us Good Jesus! Good Jesus came! Good Jesus came …He overcame, deprived, and conquered the world … for us!*

Child of God, Jesus *is* The Conqueror, the ***"Good"*** Teacher ... not the destroyer!

God never planned ... does not want to plan ... does not need to use the devil or tragedy to teach His Children His goodness! That is positively opposite to all Jesus is, and brainless thinking!

This kind of thinking sounds good to the religious mind, but it is bold face lies of the devil!

Again, God does not need to use the ways of the devil to teach us His love or goodness!

Remember, if what you think or hear doesn't line up with God's Word or His Love for you in His Word, it is a bold face lie of the devil!

OR, it is IDLE words!

Jesus is our Healer ... not our destroyer!

Jesus is our Provider ... not our depriver!

Jesus is our Giver ... not our taker!

Can you imagine a good parent coming home, being greeted by their sweet little child, and then the next thing you know, POW ... out of nowhere, that parent knocks that precious child right in the head! Next, that parent says, *"I knocked you in the head so you'll learn to know how much I love you!"*

Or, that parent sees their child getting ready to run into ongoing traffic in the street and says, *"Run on sweetheart, it's okay, you'll learn once that truck hits you!"*

Or, worse yet, that parent hears their hungry child ask for food and says, *"Now little darlin' you just lick that old moldy rotten bread, it's good enough for you!"*

Honey, when we *understand we have* God's Word, His giving Love, His Provision in His Anointed Authority working inside us, we'll be greatly surprised how much more blessed and wonderful living can be.

Never again do you or I, with our thinking, our eyes, ears, mouth or our actions, need to agree (give permission) to the devil to rob us, and wreck our lives!

In Jesus, you need NEVER, ever again, live or speak doubt, or negatively!

Never again do we have to speak or act negatively, and give the devil any authority over our lives through accepting sickness or tragedy or unwise choices!

Child of God,
it is a monumental tragedy
to *accept* living in fear, doubt, poverty,
abuse, sickness, despair, *and* defeat.

In Jesus, you are a Family member of God's Family! You belong to the most powerful Family in this Universe!

In Jesus, you have an irrevocable, massive, extravagant Inheritance from your Father! You are God's abundantly provided for, Beloved, protected Child!

In Jesus you have complete authority and dominion over every circumstance that surrounds you!

God never intended for His Children or His Church to be weak, sick, ignorant, suffering, starving, and struggling.

The Body of Christ is designed ... commanded ... to be giving, strong, courageous! We are to be filled with Jesus in the positive Word of God! We are His Bright Light and Love in the darkest of places!   Luke 11:33-36

As we *meditate* on God's Word, we are like a tree planted by the river, growing, prospering and flourishing in abundance!
                                                                    Psalms 1:2, 3

Negative, faith-less confessions give the enemy authority ... an edge into our life! Negative, faith-less confessions destroy our lives, families, and our churches!

You are accountable to Jesus, *not* the devil, or the world!

KICK THE DEVIL OUT! Look up and SPEAK God's faithful, forceful, positive Words of authority over your situation just like Jesus did! Read, read, read God's promises in Deuteronomy 28:1-18.

Stand on God's Word no matter what anything *looks* like! **YES, "*YOU* CAN STAND ON GOD'S WORD NO MATTER WHAT!"**

Keep the devil in his defeated place! Tell the devil to bow down to worship the Lord God! Tell him he is to serve the Lord God just like Jesus told him. Tell him you worship only your Good God!

Tell the devil ... *"GET LOST"!*

In Jesus, you are free. In Jesus, you can stop listening to the devil's nonsense and made up lies. In Jesus, stop listening to the enemy or anyone he's speaking through!

In Jesus, stop listening to anyone who tries to steal your hope!

Stop listening to anyone who confuses you or wants to rob you of your freedom to live abundantly in peace *and* well-being *in Jesus*.

Listen to God's love! Look up His Word that tells you exactly what to do about every circumstance in your life.

Listen *only* to God!

Jesus said, *"Only aim at and strive for and seek His way of doing and being right, and all these things shall be supplied to you also. Do not be seized with alarm and struck with fear, little flock, FOR IT IS YOUR FATHER'S GOOD PLEASURE TO GIVE YOU THE KINGDOM."*
Luke 12:31, 32

Do you see it! What is God's Way of doing and being right? Isn't His Way for us to receive His love … to walk in His love …. To give the Truth and love of Jesus to a hurting, suffering world? YES! YES! YES — Father God is faithful!

It is His good pleasure … His blessing … to give us His Kingdom!
Luke 12:32

His abundant provisions and His Kingdom — His abundant Love — His freedom from *all* bondages — IS JESUS!

God is able *and* willing! He gives ALL!

JESUS IS ALL! Abundant food, clothes, *spiritual* abundance, health, mental, emotional, intellectual and physical and financial abundance! All is ours, in Jesus! Father longs for us to have ALL of Him ... ALL of His Kingdom!

ALL His Love! ALL His provisions! ALL His protection!

ALL His grace, mercy, love, joy, peace ... forgiveness ...

ALL ... my friends ... ALL!
JESUS IS ALL!

FATHER GOD IS FAITHFUL,
ALL GIVING ... AN ALL *LOVING* FATHER!

Just for starters, let's read Acts 20:32; 1 Corinthians 10:13; 2 Corinthians 9:8; Ephesians 3:20; Hebrews 7:25.

Can we imagine what our world will be like when we as Brothers and Sisters in Christ are all acting *in unity* in ALL God's love? We can start now and get ready ... that day is nearing!

Ephesians 1:18-23; 3:16-21 and Philippians 4:19 give us a dynamic clear picture of Father God's riches in glory He has already given us!

"And my God will liberally supply (fill to the full) your every need according to His riches in glory in Christ Jesus."

Keep flooding the eyes of your heart with the Light of Jesus and His glory … His loving, rich, and saving Word.

God is faithful! He has already provided for our every need for us! He desires to bless us … to protect us! He meets our every need according to *all* His riches in glory!

God's *all* in His glory is some pretty big riches!

Jesus gave ALL!

Let's receive … let's give … HIS ALL!

Yes, *you have all* in your Lord Jesus *and* His loving, powerful Word! **Jesus is God's Faithful, Loving Word!**

Who God *says* Jesus is … *is* Who Jesus is!

**Who God is … who He *says* you are …
is who you are!**

What God *says* He'll do … He does!

God's Hands are full *with* His power, His patience, His protection!

Honey, Father God told Moses to tell the people in Egypt that *"I AM"* had sent Moses to them.

And what did Moses have to do? He only needed to believe! Then, go forth to act on what God said for him to do!

Let's grasp the truth of the awesome ability of our Father God as *"I AM!"*

God is able! God's Words are words of hope - victory!

God says in Isaiah 41:13; 49:16 that He personally has us carved in the very palms of His Hands of power and provision and protection! He says He'll never leave us or forget us!

And, if ever, should your faith weaken and you start to fear or doubt or you forget you are carved in the very palms of God's Hands, just stop … ASK Jesus to help you … to forgive you! Instantly, ask Jesus to deliver you from whatever temptation you're being offered to fear or doubt! Jesus is your immediate Deliverer, and the Forgiver!

Jesus prays forgiving!
He immediately forgives!
He forgets every weakness!

Remember, any weakness remaining in the natural human flesh part of us does not change the power of Christ alive inside us in our born again, re-created, spirit man!

Which choice are you going to stand on and live in? You can choose Death … or Life! You can choose Death … to live in the fearful, natural defeated flesh man! Or, you can choose Life … you can choose to live in your victorious, courageous God nature … your re-created spiritual man?   Deuteronomy 30:19; Proverbs 18:21

The devil is Death … **JESUS IS LIFE!**

Let's choose to walk and live in who God says we are in Jesus! With Jesus we are the redeemed, victorious born again, re-created spirit man or woman of God ... He says we are!

Let's choose Life! Let's choose to live in Jesus in Great God's Spirit alive in us! Let's choose to live in His written, powerful, spoken victory Words for us! LET'S CHOOSE LIFE!

Let's choose Jesus ...
Let's choose God's Word!

Jesus is faithful!
Jesus is patient!

Patience is consistent faith, never changing — Jesus is faithful, patient and He prays! His patience (consistent faith) is in us!

Jesus prays for us! He has provided that should we weaken (like Peter) we can " ... *turn, and* **strengthen,** *and* **establish** *our brother."*

Patience is consistent faith!

Child of God, patience *is* consistent faith. *Jesus says* you have His consistent faith! Use it!

Jesus is patient because He believes ...
He knows
He has His Father God's powerful Word *and* ability to back Him up!

Jesus knows by choice and experience that we can walk in Father God's Word, and His Love living inside us!

Jesus *knows* **we can be His example of Father's well healed, made whole, Beloved Sons and Daughters. We are His very own protected, Beloved Children.**

> *"... God is faithful and He will strengthen (you) and set you on a firm foundation and guard you from the evil (one)."*
> 2 Thessalonians 3:3

1 Corinthians 1:9 tells us how faithful our Father is, *"God is faithful (reliable, trustworthy, and therefore ever true to His promise, and He can be depended on); by Him you were called into companionship and participation with His Son, Jesus Christ our Lord.."*

Oh Glory to God! YES! God is faithful! God has called us into partnership, companionship, and participation with His Son Jesus, our Lord and Savior!

The enemy Satan has gone wild! He knows his end is near! He also knows he was eternally defeated and paralyzed 2000 years ago by Jesus!

And no matter how wild Satan gets, God is always greater, stronger, wiser! God will always be God over him!

Yes, Father God is eternally faithful to us!

2000 years ago and right now, God has all faith in us! He has us set on His firm foundation ... Jesus!

We are completely guarded and protected from the devil *through* Jesus! We can walk *in* Jesus and stand *in* His protection. We can walk *in* obedience to His victorious Word and glorious provisions for us.

God guards us from Satan
with Jesus ... in His eternal Love and Word!

Paul (Saul) knew firsthand that Satan, the defeated tempter, tries (baits, makes every attempt) to tempt (lure, entice) seduce you to listen to him and look away from Jesus — to look away from your faith — Satan will tempt you to look away from God's Word and His faith in you!

According to Acts 9:2-20, at one time, Paul acting in his religious and traditional training, literally slaughtered Christians! He rode shot-gun with the devil himself as he persecuted and killed Christians!

Then Paul, on the road to Damascus, had a direct encounter with Jesus that changed his life forever. A direct light from heaven flashed around him. He fell to the ground. Then, he heard a voice say to him, *"Saul, Saul, why are you persecuting Me (harassing, troubling, and molesting Me)? And Saul said, Who are You Lord? And He said, I am Jesus, Whom you are persecuting. It is dangerous and it will turn out badly for you to keep kicking against the goad (to offer vain and perilous resistance). Trembling and astonished he asked, Lord what do You desire me to do? The Lord said to him, But arise and go into the city, and you will be told what you must do."*

For 3 days Paul was blind! He had to be led into town, and he didn't eat or drink anything. The Lord said that Paul was a chosen instrument of our Lord God to go and proclaim the Name of Jesus to kings, and the descendants of Israel.

Paul, after his conversion to Christ, wrote, *"... I sent that I might learn (how you were standing the strain, and the endurance of) your faith, lest somehow the tempter had*

*tempted you and our toil (among you should prove to) be
fruitless and to no purpose.”*   1 Thessalonians 3:5

All the disciples, John, Peter, James, Thomas ... many
people heard Jesus teach! Jesus taught them about *how* He was
tempted by Satan, and how He had overcome Satan's
temptations at the desert edge!

Jesus repeatedly taught about His love, and His Father's
Word! By God's Word, and His example His life spoke boldly,
loud and clear of His trust, strength and courage in His Father
God's Word!

Jesus was fully equipped as the Supreme Over-comer! He
consistently decided to stand, and trust in His Fathers Word! He
always spoke and He acted on Father's Word, strength, and
love!   John 5:19

We too are equipped! We too can trust completely, and
depend on Jesus in God's Love, and His word! Satan can't
touch us!

Jesus took great pleasure in coming to give us His entire
Self! We *have* Jesus!

Father God takes great pleasure to abundantly provide us
His entire Kingdom Life!

We can receive ... walk, and run in His Kingdom Life
totally free of worry, sickness, disease, despair, loss, and lack.

We can receive more in Psalms 23 , 91; Psalms 118 ...
Psalms 103 ... of the power, and love of God in Jesus for us.

Yes, Glory to God, in the ability of Jesus living inside us,
we can read, hear, believe, receive, speak (confess), and act
(walk) in all God's Love, and Word for each of us!

What a credible Savior, Lord, Good Shepherd, Conqueror, and Deliverer in Love we have!

JESUS *IS*
THE TRUTH ... OUR TRUTH
THE HEALER ... OUR HEALER!

Never again ... give in ...
to the liar devil!   Ephesians 4:27

Never give up your Jesus!

NEVER — NEVER — GIVE UP!

NEVER, NEVER LET ANYTHING
SO SORROW YOU ... TO ROB YOU
OF YOUR JOY IN JESUS ...
OR HIS WORD ...
OR HIS LOVE ...
FOR YOU!   Ezekiel 36:26-28

Never forget,
SATAN IS THE *DEFEATED* **TEMPTER ...**

You are never tempted
beyond the ability of your Deliverer, Jesus!

Remember, your eyes are Jesus' Eyes ...
Matthew 20:34
Your hands are His Hands ...
1 Timothy 2:8
Your mouth is His Mouth ...
Romans 10:10, 11

Your ears are His Ears …
Isaiah 50:4, 5
Your feet are His Feet …
Ephesians 6:15
Your arms are His Arms …
Isaiah 53
Your mind is His Mind …
1 Corinthians 2:16
Your life is His Life …
John 6:35; Colossians 3:3
You have the Wisdom of God!
Psalms 111:10
You are the Love of God!
Romans 8:35-39

**Look at God's Life living inside you …
Look through the Beautiful, Forgiving,
loving, faithful eyes of your Jesus
and *see* your Lord Jesus
alive in your life!**

**The Love
of your *Jesus is in you!***

Jesus … in you … is everything!

**<u>YOU CAN TRUST JESUS
ETERNALLY!</u>**

**YOUR FATHER GOD … YOUR JESUS
ARE
FOREVER FAITHFUL!**   Isaiah 40:8, 9

Prayer for Salvation
and Baptism in the Holy Spirit

Heavenly Father, I come to You in the Name of Jesus. Your Word says, *"Whosoever shall call on the name of the Lord shall be saved"* (Acts 2:21), so I call on You Lord.

I pray asking Jesus to come into my heart and be Lord over my life, according to Romans 10:9 *"Because if you acknowledge and confess with your lips that Jesus is Lord and in your heart believe that God raised Him from the dead, you will be saved."*

I do that now. I confess that Jesus is Lord, and I believe in my heart that God raised Him from the dead. I am now re-born! I am a Christian—a child of Almighty God! I am saved!

You also said in Your Word Lord, *"If you then, evil as you are, know how to give good gifts to your children, how much more will your heavenly Father give the Holy Spirit to those who ask and continue to ask Him!"* (Luke 11:13). Lord, I am also asking You to fill me with the Holy Spirit. Holy Spirit, rise up within me as I praise God. I fully expect to speak with other tongues as You give me utterance (Acts 2:4).

Begin now! Praise God! Praise Him for filling you with His Love and Holy Spirit. Let your voice rise up in praise to Father God in the voice the Holy Spirit gives you. Use your voice to worship and praise Him in heavenly language.

Make every day a day of blessing! Father God has given you Jesus! He has given you His Word …a great blessing of His Love, His mercy, forgiveness, and life eternal with Him. You are a born-again, re-created, Spirit-filled believer. You'll never be the same!

Now, find a strong, good Word of God preaching church! Become a part of a church family who will love you and care for you as you care for them.

We need to be joined to each other. Like a tightly woven rope, it is God's plan for us to be strong in unity together!

Signed_____

Date_____

<u>CONCLUSION</u>

**Read God's victorious conquering Words in this book
over again, and again, and again!**

*Study God's great love and Word for you in
God's Cookin' and the Devil's Well Done!*

*Give away this rich book of victory
and love in Jesus to a friend!*

**Father God's Love and Word guarantees you His joy!
He is your mercy, *and* strength.**

You *can't* change your life!
Jesus *can ... and He will ...* change your life!

LISTEN TO JESUS! LISTEN TO HIS LOVE!
Receive FATHER'S WORD ... YOU WILL EASILY
RECOGNIZE (EXPOSE) THE *defeated* DEVIL!

AS YOU LINE UP YOUR MIND, YOUR MOUTH, *and*
ACTIONS *with* GOD'S LOVE *and* HIS WORD FOR YOU,
SATAN'S LIES *and* SCHEMES ARE EXPOSED!

AS YOU LEARN TO LIVE IN JESUS ...
LIVING IN GOD'S LOVE *and* WORD FOR YOU ...
YOU WILL LIVE IN HIS ABUNDANCE!

Go ahead, STAND, WALK,
and RUN VICTORIOUSLY *IN JESUS!*

Praise the Lord ... Encourage yourself ... Encourage others!

Look for: THE FOUR (4) KEYS TO SUPER PRAISE, and
VICTORY OVER LOSS *and* ANGER in ROSE's booklet
titled:

Love *Is* on the Throne *and* He's Not Nervous!

ORDER TODAY

Books, Booklets, Tapes, CD's Available from

Rose Leibundguth Ministries

Learn today how to victoriously live your life in the courage you already have with Jesus … call or write …

**order these and more anointed, dynamic
HEART *and* LIFE-CHANGING
powerful books …**

GOD's COOKIN' *and the* **DEVIL's WELL DONE**
LOVE IS ON THE THRONE and HE's NOT NERVOUS
JESUS IS LORD SURROUNDS YOU
DANCING WITH *THE KING*
DRESSED TO WIN
FEASTING ON GOD's WORD
YOU ARE GOD's BELOVED
YOU ARE GOD's CREATION
JESUS IS YOUR DEFENDER

The Lone Ranger had a Tonto (unity in the community)
Holy Bologny (sit down - eat with Jesus)
ONE BABIES DEAD, but, FIVE ARE ALIVE
        (keeping your eyes on Jesus)
When the Devil Presses in - YOU PRESS ON
You are More Than A Conqueror
Hunger to be Satisfied
Christ in You
SET FREE - SET FREE - SET FREE
The Love Life is Worth Living
Patience is Consistent Faith
Love Overcomes Everything
You can Never Stumble or Fall
Cast Your Good Bread on the Water
Give More … MORE & MORE
Plant Seeds - Remove Pressure
What Being Rich Really Means
                    AND MORE!

ORDER TODAY

Music & Teaching Tapes Available from
Rose Leibundguth Ministries

MUSIC   (Cassettes & CD's)

The Rose   (Vocal Music)

Mercy's Voice   (Beautiful Orchestrated Piano)

Song Titles: In the Garden
I Need Thee Every Hour
Have Thyne Own Way, Lord
Precious Lord Take My Hand
Jesus Loves Me
Mercy's Voice
Lisa's Song
He
One Heart
The Wind Beneath My Wings

VICTORY TEACHING TAPES

"You Are Loved"
"The Devil *is* Your Slave" (2 tape series)
"Set Free Indeed" (3 tape series)
"God's Will For You"
"GO - GO - GO" (to the other side) (3 tape series)
"Forgive *and* Forget"
"Praise Him Instead"

Rose Leibundguth Ministries

Learn more about
Mercy House / Rose Leibundguth Ministries
Healing Hearts Victory Campaign Meetings,
or to order these and other excellent
victory ministry products

Mercy House
ROSE LEIBUNDGUTH MINISTRIES
BOX M
BURGIN, KENTUCKY 40310
859-748-9961 / fax 859-748-6060
e-mail — rose8@kih.net
www.mercyhouserocks.org

For more information on *Mercy House*
Call 859 - 748-9961

Your Partnership
with this worldwide work of

Mercy House
ROSE LEIBUNDGUTH MINISTRIES
is valuable for thousands
and appreciated by all!

Rose Leibundguth